OSCAR ROMERO AND THE COMMUNION OF THE SAINTS

# OSCAR ROMERO

## AND

# THE COMMUNION
# OF THE SAINTS

*A Biography*

REVISED EDITION

SCOTT WRIGHT

*With Photos by Octavio Duran*

ORBIS BOOKS

**Maryknoll, New York 10545**

# ORBIS BOOKS
**Maryknoll, New York 10545**

**Fathers and Brothers MARYKNOLL**
TOGETHER IN GOD'S MISSION OF MERCY

Founded in 1970, Orbis Books endeavors to publish works that enlighten the mind, nourish the spirit, and challenge the conscience. The publishing arm of the Maryknoll Fathers and Brothers, Orbis seeks to explore the global dimensions of the Christian faith and mission, to invite dialogue with diverse cultures and religious traditions, and to serve the cause of reconciliation and peace. The books published reflect the views of their authors and do not represent the official position of the Maryknoll Society. To learn more about Maryknoll and Orbis Books, please visit our website at www.maryknollsociety.org.

**Library of Congress Cataloging-in-Publication Data**

Wright, Scott, 1950-

Oscar Romero and the communion of the saints : a biography / Scott Wright ; with photos by Octavio Duran.

p. cm.

Includes bibliographical references.

ISBN 978-1-57075-839-3 (pbk.)

ISBN 978-1-62698-185-0 (pbk. rev. ed.)

1. Romero, Oscar A. (Oscar Arnulfo), 1917-1980. 2. Catholic Church—El Salvador—Bishops—Biography. I. Title.

BX4705.R669W75 2009

282'.7284092—dc22

[B]

2009010653

*Dedicated*
*to Dean Brackley, S.J.*
*1946-2011*
*and*
*Jim Harney*
*1940–2008*

*Faithful companions on the journey,*
*who taught their friends to live in*
*solidarity with the crucified of the planet.*

*Thank you.*

*Children of El Salvador, 1984. Photo by Jim Harney*

*Easter is itself now the cry of victory.*
*No one can quench that life that Christ has resurrected.*
*Neither death nor all the banners of death and hatred*
*raised against Him and against His church can prevail.*
*He is the victorious one!*
*Just as He will thrive in an unending Easter,*
*so we must accompany Him in a Lent and a Holy Week*
*of cross, sacrifice, and martyrdom.*
*As He said, blessed are they who are not scandalized*
*by His cross.*

—Oscar Romero, *The Violence of Love*
MARCH 23, 1980

# CONTENTS

# Acknowledgments

This book was written in gratitude. Just as it takes a village to raise a child, it takes a community to remember a story and embody a tradition of Christian witness and martyrdom. I would like to express my thanks to those who have made this book possible.

My deepest gratitude goes to the people of El Salvador, and to those Salvadoran friends and pastoral workers from whom I first heard the stories of Oscar Romero in the refugee camps, villages, and basic Christian communities I accompanied during the years of the war. Your stories and witness are at the very heart of this book.

In particular, I thank Father Jon Sobrino, SJ,[1] and Monseñor Ricardo Urioste,[2] for your faithful remembrance of Oscar Romero; María Julia Hernández, former director of the Archdiocese of San Salvador's Legal Aid Office, and Rufina Amaya, the lone survivor of the El Mozote massacre—both now deceased—for your faithful witness to human rights; and Miguel Cavada and Denyse Brunet of Equipo Maiz, for your labor of love and generosity in sharing many of the precious photos of Romero that appear in this book.

I thank Robert Ellsberg, the publisher of Orbis Books, for your encouragement, guidance, and faithful witness over many years, promoting the remembrance of the lives of the saints and martyrs; Octavio Duran, personal photographer to Romero, for your inspired pictures, stories, and collaboration; and Marie Dennis, for your gracious invitation to work on this project.

Much of this book travels a path already opened by previous biographers and storytellers, among whom I wish to thank: James Brockman, SJ, author of *Romero: A Life*;[3] María López Vigil and Kathy Ogle, author and translator of *Oscar Romero: Memories in Mosaic*;[4] Eugene Palumbo and Dean Brackley, SJ; Margaret Swedish and Renny Golden; Marie Dennis and Joe Nangle, OFM; Eileen Purcell and Jose Artiga; Jim Barnett, OP, and Tom Howarth; and my compadres Peter O'Driscoll and Christine Reesor.

I also thank many dear and unnamed friends who share a love for Archbishop Romero and for the Salvadoran martyrs, and who continue to be for me that nourishing community known as the "communion of saints." In particular I thank Peter Hinde, O.Carm., and Betty Campbell, RSM.

Finally, my deepest gratitude goes to my life partner, Jean Stokan, and to our daughter Maura, for your constant support and encouragement, and for your friendship and steadfast love, for which I am ever grateful.

# Preface

Blessed Oscar Romero: Martyr for Justice, Martyr for Love

*Oscar Romero and the Communion of Saints was first published in 2009, six years before Romero's beatification. We offer this preface as a testimony to the significance of his life and martyrdom to the church and to the world.*

On May 23, 2015, Archbishop Oscar Romero of El Salvador was officially recognized as "blessed" by the Vatican in a ceremony in San Salvador that marked the conclusion of a long journey. Romero, the beloved pastor, prophet, and martyr, was assassinated at the altar while celebrating Mass, March 24, 1980. At the very moment in the ceremony that officially declared Archbishop Romero "Blessed," bells rang out to celebrate the occasion, and the eyes of the crowd turned upward to witness a rare and beautiful rainbow halo around the midday sun. It seemed a fitting recognition, or providential "sign" and validation of the significance of Romero's beatification, and the suffering and sacrifice of the Salvadoran people who had already declared Romero a "saint" and a "martyr" thirty-five years before.

By the sheer number of people present at the beatification—by some counts as many as 300,000—there was little doubt that Romero has, in words attributed to him before his death, "risen in his people." Young and old, those who remembered the suffering and violence of the war as though it were yesterday, and those who had only heard stories of those years from parents and grandparents, gathered from the furthest corners of El Salvador, Latin America, and around the world to commemorate this day. They embodied, by their presence, the words of the psalm read during the celebration: *"Those who go out weeping, bearing the seed for sowing, shall come home with shouts of joy, carrying their sheaves."* (Psalm 126:6)

This new edition of *Oscar Romero and the Communion of Saints* is dedicated to Jim Harney, a photojournalist whose pictures from El Salvador appear throughout this book, and to Dean Brackley, a Jesuit who responded to the call to come to El Salvador after the murder of the six Jesuit priests on November 16, 1989. Dean remained there until his death on October 16, 2011. A few days later, *America* published one of his essays entitled, "Meeting the Victim, Loving the Poor." In it, Brackley narrates the journey of thousands of people he met during their pilgrimages to El Salvador, and what happened to them—and him—in their encounter with the poor:

> Waves of foreign delegations have come to El Salvador in recent years. The pilgrims deplane a little anxious, vaguely dreading what awaits them. They know that the people are very poor. They have heard of massacres and bombings of the past and the hunger and sickness of the present. . . . On the one hand, the visitors spend much of their time in El Salvador wondering why these poor people are smiling. The people are glad they came and receive them with open arms. On the other hand, if the pilgrims listen to the stories of flight

from the army, torture and death squads, and since the war, of unspeakable hardship and premature death, the victims will break their hearts. And that, after all, is the main reason the pilgrims have come. (*America*, October 19, 2011)

Many people, however, would prefer that the memory of Archbishop Romero and the people of El Salvador be forgotten. For those who lived through the turbulent years of the civil war (1980–1992), they remember how Archbishop Romero was bitterly attacked and labeled as a communist and a terrorist by the wealthy and by the military, and considered with suspicion as an unworthy ally by the Reagan administration and by many conservative sectors of the church. What is so impressive is that Romero is as alive today in his people and throughout the world as he was when he was archbishop of San Salvador. In the words of one of the songs popularized by the Christian base communities following Romero's assassination, "They can kill the prophet, but not the voice of justice." The chorus concludes, "They will impose silence, but history will not be silent."

Not since the murder of Thomas Becket, Archbishop of Canterbury, in 1170 has the witness of an archbishop provoked such "hatred of the faith." Becket was killed for defending the rights of the church before the king; Romero for defending the rights of the poor before the oligarchy and military. As many poor Salvadorans say, "He was killed because he spoke the truth and defended the poor." These words, often cited by Jon Sobrino, SJ, are at the heart of what it means to say that Archbishop Romero was "a martyr for love," the somewhat controversial motto chosen by the archdiocese for his beatification. "In truth, Monseñor Romero is [a saint] for all of us," an editorial from the Jesuit University of Central America (UCA) affirmed, shortly before his beatification. "But one cannot hide the fact that he was martyred out of hatred of the faith and, because of that, as Pope Francis has noted, he became and is a martyr for justice. He was martyred because he faithfully followed, without fail, in the steps of Jesus in choosing decisively to side with the victims of injustice and violence. This is why he is a saint."

The day before Archbishop Romero was murdered, in a homily broadcast to the nation that sealed his fate, he called on the Salvadoran government to end the slaughter of its people: "In the name of God, and in the name of this long-suffering people, whose laments rise to heaven every day more tumultuous, I beseech you, I beg you, I command you in the name of God: 'Stop the repression!'" Now, more than three decades later, El Salvador is still a land of lights and shadows, of a past that remains to be healed and a future still uncertain; but on the day of Romero's beatification, it was a present full of joy.

For many people throughout the world, the beatification of Oscar Romero is a sign of the kind of church that Pope Francis desires, the church to which Archbishop Romero bore witness during his lifetime: "a poor church for the poor." Comparing Romero to Moses, Pope Francis said: "In times of difficult coexistence, Archbishop Romero knew how to lead, defend, and protect his flock, remaining faithful to the Gospel and in communion with the whole church." But it is not enough to remember the past; we must commit our lives to the future. In the words of Noemi Ortíz, a base community member who worked with Romero as his secretary, "Our challenge today is not only to know Romero's thoughts, his homilies, his actions, but to speak and act as he did among our people. . . . The martyrs will live as long as we do not let them die and forget their witness."

The beatification of Archbishop Romero, then, is not the end but the beginning of a journey of sanctification, not only of his life, but much more of the life of "a poor church for the poor" that is born anew, as it was on the day of Pentecost, of the blood of the martyrs. Perhaps the greatest legacy of Archbishop Romero is that he embodied truth, justice, and mercy as the heart of the Gospel and was a living witness to what it means to be a Christian today. In death as in life, Romero bore witness to a church committed to mercy and to justice, to the liberation of the poor from every oppression, and to a love that knows no limits in its zeal to protect and defend the poor: "No one has greater love than this, to lay down one's life for one's friends" (John 15:13).

Linda Panetta/SOA Watch

# Introduction

"Oscar Romero . . . *Presente!*"

So the procession began. Twenty thousand walked solemnly, six abreast, lifting their crosses as the names of each of the martyrs from Latin America was called out from the stage. Since 1990, this solemn ritual has become a tradition for those who remember the victims and the martyrs, and gather every November before the gates of the School of the Americas at Fort Benning, Georgia, to protest the military training of Latin American armies responsible for those assassinations.

"Ignacio Ellacuría . . . *Presente!*"

What was special about this year's commemoration[5] was the presence of Jon Sobrino, SJ, theologian and colleague of the six Jesuit martyrs, their housekeeper, and her daughter. Nearly twenty years after their assassination by soldiers trained at the School of the Americas, and nearly thirty years after Romero's assassination, Father Sobrino had been invited by Pax Christi USA to join thousands to commemorate their lives and to proclaim the power of their witness.

By late morning, thousands of names of the victims had been read, and crosses bearing their names now covered the chain-link fence of the military base in a sea of white wood. Tears mingled with cries of the names of the victims, as the three-hour procession slowly passed by the gates of the military base, and the voices of twenty thousand responded: *"Presente!"*

We live in a time of saints and martyrs. The twentieth century created more victims of war and terror, but it also gave birth to more saints and martyrs than any other century. The martyrs and the witness of these humble men and women lay a claim upon our lives and forever enable us to dream the impossible, to bring forth justice, to imagine peace, and to cross divides of class, race, gender, religion, and nationality in ways that bind us together as one human family—or, in the words of another martyr, Dr. Martin Luther King, Jr., as the "beloved community."

This book is about the Salvadoran bishop Oscar Romero, who was assassinated March 24, 1980, at the altar while celebrating Mass. Romero is a prophet, saint, and martyr for our time. His death, like that of Jesus of Nazareth, was the dramatic conclusion of a life lived in fidelity to God that brought him into conflict with the political authorities of his nation. His life, too, resembled in many ways the life of Jesus of Nazareth, as noted by Martin Maier, SJ.[6]

Oscar Romero and Jesus of Nazareth were born into conditions of poverty, in the province of a small and insignificant country. Both lived a life of profound intimacy with God and prayed by night. They both learned the trade of a carpenter. For both, the assassination of a good friend became a decisive event in their lives. They became public figures through their preaching, proclaiming the goodness of God and announcing the coming of the kingdom of God as a new order of love among all people.

Both took sides with the poor and those who were socially excluded. Following the tradition of the prophets of Israel, they denounced injustice and corruption. In time, all of the important social groups were allied against them. They were accused of being traitors who tried to upset the established order. Both confronted the imperialist powers of their day, and their public life lasted a mere three years.

These comparisons have not been lost on the poor of El Salvador. One peasant refugee says:

> Monseñor Romero was like a Salvadoran Jesus Christ . . . When they killed him, we were very sad because we thought that everything had ended. But later we saw that his spirit gave us strength to resist oppression. For that reason we also believe more now in Jesus Christ.[7]

The poor of El Salvador have never forgotten Oscar Romero, perhaps because he never forgot them. They were at the heart of his pastoral accompaniment, his proclamation of the Gospel, his prophetic defense of their lives, his martyrdom. "The glory of God," he said, "is the living poor person."[8]

It is a bit daunting to tell the story of a saint. What makes it less so is remembering the people from whom I first heard the stories about Romero, those humble campesinos[9] who loved and revered him, because he first loved and defended them: the poor of El Salvador.

I met Archbishop Romero once, in 1979, after a talk he had given to the press at the Latin American Bishops' Conference in Puebla, Mexico.[10] I simply shook his hand and thanked him. I really came to know him through his people, in the refugee camps, rural villages, conflictive areas, and poor parishes of El Salvador during the years of the war. I worked as a pastoral worker for the Catholic church for most of the decade of the 1980s, and came to know and love Oscar Romero through his people.

Since leaving El Salvador in 1990, I have always felt that because of the years I lived there, the poor have a particular claim on our lives. Partly, it is from a sense of Christian duty and solidarity not to forget the suffering—a suffering that continues today due to poverty, exclusion, and violence—and the still unfulfilled hopes and dreams of the people for a dignified life and for greater justice and freedom for their children.

But even more than duty, it is profound gratitude that is at the heart of this remembrance and claim. I received so much from the people of El Salvador—from their goodness and their strength, their hospitality and their faith, their generosity and their courage in struggling for justice—that I am inspired to give back in equal measure in whatever way I can. This book is a humble attempt to do just that: to communicate the same values and inspire the same commitment that Romero's life offers all who take the time to learn his story.

Archbishop Romero was shaped by the Second Vatican Council and later by the Latin American Bishops' Conference at Medellín; but it was not always so. His formation as a priest preceded by twenty years the Second Vatican Council, and while he accepted the changes of the council, he initially resisted the conclusions of the Latin American bishops at Medellín.

What happened to change him is, in part, the subject of this book. Whether his "conversion" was sudden or gradual, there is little doubt that he was transformed by his contact with the poor and, in particular, by the assassination of his friend Father Rutilio Grande, SJ, which happened just twenty days after Romero had become archbishop of San Salvador.

Scott Wright

Romero began to see the world with "new eyes," to see it from the perspective of the poor and with an eye to the structural causes of poverty; he began to respond to the suffering of the poor with "eyes of compassion," demanding profound and urgent transformations of the social structures, and promoting greater participation of the poor in those changes and greater justice.

What joins Romero's life to our own in a relationship of love is what joins the living and the dead in a common bond that the tradition of the church speaks of as the communion of saints. For Christians, according to Elizabeth Johnson, the communion of saints is rooted in "the memory and hope of the Christian community" and "grounded on the foundational narrative and witness of the life, death, and resurrection of Jesus Christ."[11]

Such a framework works well for understanding the witness and legacy of Oscar Romero and his solidarity with the poor. What Archbishop Romero has done—along with the many generous and humble people in El Salvador who gave their lives out of love for the poor and for justice—is to transform this symbol of the communion of saints into one that speaks to our times by linking faith, hope, and love to justice, and by providing a living example of what Stanley Hauerwas calls "performing the faith," bearing witness to God's love and God's justice for the poor.

But it is important to remember that Romero's holiness stands on holy ground, drenched in martyrs' blood. Jon Sobrino alluded to this when he spoke in the chapel of the UCA martyrs on the first day of peace in El Salvador, February 1, 1992. As he reflected on the meaning of that day,

Sobrino said, "All of El Salvador is holy ground, because when great love and great suffering converge, then we are standing on holy ground."

I think the people of the United States and El Salvador shall forever be united by bonds of blood and martyrdom, on account of the witness of our own martyrs who were killed December 2, 1980, just nine months after Romero's assassination.

I mean, of course, the four church women, Maura Clarke, Ita Ford, Dorothy Kazel, and Jean Donovan—two Maryknoll sisters, one Ursuline sister, and one lay person—who accompanied the very poor that Romero faithfully defended.

Shortly before he was assassinated, Archbishop Romero was asked by a foreign journalist, "What message would you like to give to the peoples of the world?" He replied that helping the world understand the true situation in El Salvador was crucial, and he added: "Don't forget that we are people, and here we are dying, and fleeing to the mountains to survive."[12]

As we look out on the world today, on this, the thirtieth anniversary of his martyrdom—a world marked by profound divides of wealth and misery, devastating wars and genocide, and an ecosystem in danger of collapse—I hope that we may be mindful of Romero's challenge to us—"Don't forget, we are people"—and find ways to respond with solidarity, justice, and compassion.

Have we forgotten the poor?

We must ask ourselves that question when our nation's wars and bank bailouts reach into the trillions of dollars, while we offer the world's poor and our own poor a pittance.

We must ask ourselves that question—and be honest with ourselves and honest with reality—when we look with compassion at the victims in Iraq and Afghanistan, and feel indignation at policies and structures that justify torture and institutionalize a "war on terror."

We must ask ourselves that question when we see the fences and walls going up on the U.S.–Mexico border and witness the night raids on immigrant homes and workplaces, or when we turn a deaf ear to the cries of the victims of Hurricane Katrina or a blind eye to the unfulfilled dreams of people of color still waiting for justice in our city ghettos, prisons, and reservations.

"Don't forget, we are people," the poor and the victims of war remind us, "and we are still fleeing to the mountains and across borders just trying to survive."

Truly, Romero's life inspires many, many people throughout the world, Christians and non-Christians alike, by his prophetic defense of the poor and by his witness of martyrdom. But we must never forget the most essential thing, that for which he gave his life: to work so that the poor have life. The glory of God, he reminds us, is that the poor live.

We are truly surrounded by "a cloud of witnesses" (Hebrews 12:1) who cheer us on "to run with perseverance the race that is set before us," keeping our eyes fixed on Jesus who endured the cross for our sake and the sake of the joy to come. We are not alone, and though the journey and struggle for justice be hard, it leads to that beloved community of peace and justice to which we all aspire.

Together with Oscar Romero—and with all of the saints and martyrs who have gone before—we belong to that communion of saints, and with them we are called to become "friends of God and friends of prophets,"[13] even if it cost us our comforts and our lives.

So we can say with confidence: "Oscar Romero . . . *Presente*!"

OSCAR ROMERO AND THE COMMUNION OF THE SAINTS

# Friends of God and Prophets

*From generation to generation, she passes into holy
souls and makes them friends of God, and prophets.*

—*Wisdom 7:27*

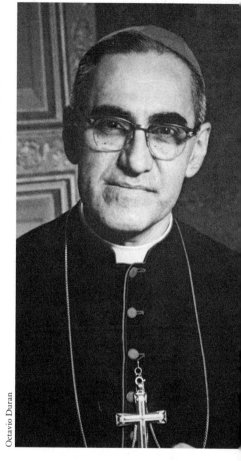

Octavio Duran

The year 2010 marks the thirtieth anniversary of the martyrdom of Oscar Romero, pastor and prophet to the Salvadoran people, and Archbishop of San Salvador from 1977 to 1980. Today, Romero is revered throughout the world as a saint, though his canonization is still a work in progress.

Jon Sobrino, perhaps more than anyone else, has helped to convey the significance and legacy of Archbishop Romero to the world. He writes:

> The word of Monseñor Romero is, like the truth and because it is true, "always old and always new," as St. Augustine said. Today as much as yesterday, that word keeps casting light on the reality of our world, unmasking lies, demanding justice and conversion. With martyrs like this, there is hope for humanity.[14]

To truly understand the life and witness of Oscar Romero, we must understand the land called El Salvador and its people. Romero's life cannot be understood apart from the Salvadoran people, their culture and their history. Romero was especially rooted in the life of the poor whom he loved. His life among the poor, during one of the most turbulent and violent epochs of Salvadoran history, brought him face to face with his people, crucified by poverty and tortured by violence. In that encounter with Christ, crucified in the poor, Romero discovered a source of life, light, and salvation for the world.

In his brief three years as Archbishop of San Salvador, Romero was eminently a pastor, showing pastoral concern for the poor and visiting them in their impoverished rural communities and marginal urban parishes. He was also an inspiring preacher, proclaiming the Good News of the Gospel each Sunday to a packed

Archbishop Romero relaxes with seminarians. (Octavio Duran)

*"I know exactly who I am, brothers. You are the ones who have to determine who you are!"*
—March 2, 1978

crowd in the metropolitan cathedral of San Salvador, the only place in the country where the truth could be named, the causes of violence identified, and the perpetrators held accountable.

In his role as a preacher, Romero took up the mantle of a prophet; he became the voice of those without voice, denouncing the slow death by oppression and the rapid death by repression in a nation marked by extremes of wealth and poverty, and violence. In the end, he became a martyr, ultimately mixing his own blood with the blood of his people and offering his life out of love for the poor.

In each of these ways—as pastor, preacher, prophet, and martyr—Oscar Romero united the love of God and the love of the poor with the heart of a mystic immersed in his people.

The Book of Wisdom speaks of wisdom passing into holy souls and making them "friends of God, and prophets." While this is surely an apt description of the life and witness of Oscar Romero, the deeper meaning of this passage may be found in the context of a holy people, "a cloud of witnesses," and the ancient symbol of the church as the communion of saints.

Elizabeth Johnson, in her book *Friends of God and Prophets*, offers a reinterpretation of this symbol as the communal practice of memory, hope, and solidarity "grounded on the foundational narrative of the life, death, and resurrection of Jesus Christ." Such a narrative is embodied in a concrete community called the church, and embedded in the Gospel stories, in our creeds, in our liturgical practices, and in the witness of the saints and martyrs. Together with "the stories of countless other women and men who have responded in vastly different ways to the Spirit's call to discipleship," the Gospel story lives on in the stories of holy souls and holy peoples. "In a particular way, the stories of the world's forgotten and unnamed resonate with the promise of the Crucified."[15]

In this book we hope to examine the life and witness of Oscar Romero within the context of his people, his people's story and history, and the communion of saints expressed in the practice of memory, hope, and solidarity that so characterized the church of San Salvador while Romero was archbishop. We begin with his own journey and deepening conversion to the God of the Crucified and Risen One, Jesus Christ, and to the crucified and risen Christ among the poor of his people.

# The Land of the Savior

On March 24, 1980, Archbishop Oscar Romero was killed by an assassin's bullet as he celebrated his last Eucharist in San Salvador. It was a death that reverberated, not only in the streets and hills of El Salvador and Central America, but throughout the world. "His death," liberation theologian Gustavo Gutiérrez remarked in one sweeping statement, "divides the recent history of the Latin American church into a before and after."[16]

Poverty for the poor of El Salvador, and the poor of Latin America, Africa, and Asia, means death, and those who do not die slowly from hunger and disease, die quickly from violence and repression. That has been the fate of the poor in El Salvador for a very long time.

In 1932, more than thirty thousand peasants were killed when they rebelled against the military dictatorship of General Maximiliano Hernández Martínez. For generations, a wealthy minority grew richer off the labor of the poor who harvested the indigo, coffee, sugarcane, and cotton produced for export, while a largely landless majority grew poorer.[17]

By the end of the 1970s, after nearly fifty years of military rule, workers, peasants, students, and teachers had organized in a multitude of grassroots organizations, bringing the nation to the brink of insurrection and civil war. The government responded with more repression, killing more than twelve thousand people in 1980 alone, the same year Archbishop Romero was assassinated. No longer able to organize nonviolently, peo-

*"My life is not mine, it is yours."*
—August 21, 1977

ple took to the hills to join rebel organizations or they fled across the border to become refugees and exiles in other countries.

In January 1981, nine months after Romero's assassination, war broke out as the FMLN (Farabundo Martí National Liberation Front) declared a general insurrection. The Salvadoran government, supported by military aid and training from the United States,[18] responded by waging a counterinsurgency war against their own people. Civilians, not insurgents, were the principal victims of this war; the poor who lived in rural areas were especially hard hit. Little attempt was made by the government to address the structural injustice that was the cause of the conflict. What reforms they attempted were secondary to the massive repression of the people.

The litany of suffering during twelve years of war (1980–1992) was dramatic: 75,000 dead, 7,000 disappeared, 1,500,000 people displaced from their homes or in exile. Major responsibility for these deaths was laid at the feet of the Salvadoran government and death squads by the United Nations Truth Commission; they accounted for 90 percent of the deaths, while the FMLN accounted for 5 percent.[19]

Initial reactions in the U.S. Congress to the Truth Commission report included a call for an immediate investigation to see whether previous administration witnesses had lied to Congress about the extent to which human rights were being violated in El Salvador.[20] In addition, the Secretary of State appointed a panel to investigate charges "that State Department officials misled Congress about atrocities by the military in El Salvador throughout the 1980s."[21]

The panel identified the core question regarding human rights policy in El Salvador as "whether the improvement of the terrible human rights situation or prosecution of the war against leftist forces should be the overriding goal of U.S. policy."[22] But it refused to acknowledge any contradiction between these two goals, and it failed to question the morality of U.S. intervention on the side of a military that systematically murdered tens of thousands of its citizens during twelve years of civil war.

Romero's assassination in 1980 drew attention to another phenomenon of the conflict: the persecution of the church. Nine months after Romero's assassination, the Salvadoran National Guard killed three North American nuns and one laywoman.

Octavio Duran

Between 1977 and 1989, a dozen and a half priests were killed, including six Jesuits assassinated along with their housekeeper and her daughter on November 16, 1989. Those responsible for the killing of Romero, the three nuns and a laywoman, and the six Jesuit priests had all been trained at the School of the Americas in Fort Benning, Georgia.[23]

On January 16, 1992, with the help of the United Nations, the Salvadoran government and the FMLN rebels signed a peace accord, effectively putting an end to the war. The Salvadoran army was purged of officers responsible for crimes, though they were quickly granted amnesty by the government. The military was reduced by half, and the FMLN was demobilized and disarmed, becoming a political party.

What has happened to the people of El Salvador since the end of the war? Many who were poor before the war are even poorer today. The poor live on the edge of life in a daily struggle to survive. Those who did not die during the war wage a daily battle against poverty, hunger, and disease. The violence of the war and death squad assassinations has given way to a more subtle, but pervasive, criminal violence and gang activity.[24]

The cost of living has risen dramatically, and so has inequality. One third of the population has migrated to the United States in search of a better life. There, many are subject to raids on their workplaces and homes, months of incarceration and separation from their families, and deportation to El Salvador.

The remarkable thing is that people still have hope, a hope which bore fruit in the March 2009 election of Mauricio Funes, the FMLN candidate for president of El Salvador. Despite the pervasive violence and daily struggle to survive, the poor in El Salvador continue to hope and to demonstrate an amazing generosity and solidarity.

Much of this hope is due to a vibrant faith and the witness of the martyrs. Twenty years after the martyrdom of the six Jesuits and two women, and thirty years after the martyrdom of Oscar Romero, the hope of the people is quite evident in the joy and vitality of their celebrations commemorating the life of the martyrs. They continue to be the people about whom Archbishop Romero remarked: "With this people it is not hard to be a good shepherd. They are a people that impel to their service us who have been called to defend their rights and to be their voice."[25]

*"With this people it is not hard to be a good shepherd."*
—November 18, 1979

# Family

Oscar Romero was born in Ciudad Barrios on August 15, 1917. His parents were Guadalupe de Jesús Galdámez and Santos Romero.
(Zoila Aurora Asturias and Eva del Carmen Asturias)

What was it that enabled a traditional pastor to become a martyr of the church? Nothing in his childhood, training for the priesthood, or his first twenty-five years as a priest offers any indication that Romero would become a prophet-martyr in his three last years as archbishop of San Salvador.

This is not an easy question to answer. Jon Sobrino writes that Archbishop Romero "did not particularly like to hear his change referred to as a conversion. And he had a point. He used to recall his humble origins. He had never known anything like wealth or abundance. His family had led a life of poverty and austerity."[26]

Oscar Romero was born August 15, 1917, into a modest family in Ciudad Barrios in the department of San Miguel, only ten miles from the Honduran border. The town, named after Gerardo Barrios, a nineteenth-century political figure, was originally known by its indigenous name, Cacahuatique. The features of the people still reflect their indigenous roots, mingled with the blood of the Spanish conquistadores to form a people and country known as El Salvador.

Oscar Romero was the son of humble parents. His father, Santos Romero, worked as the town's postmaster and telegraph operator in the morning, and cultivated cacao and coffee on a small plot of land in the afternoon.[27] He was not particularly pious, and had the required religious instruction before marrying, but he did teach Oscar to pray in early childhood. Guadalupe de Jesús Galdámez, his mother, remained close to her son until her death in 1961.

Oscar was the second of eight children in a family of six boys and two girls. His sister Zaida recalled the order: "There was Gustavo, then Oscar, Zaida, Aminta, who died when she was little, Romulo, who died when he was older, Mamerto, Arnoldo, and Gaspar."[28] Oscar was baptized May 11, 1919, in the parish of Ciudad Barrios.

The family's means were modest, and the home, like other homes in Ciudad Barrios in 1917, had no electricity. Romero's

Romero was born and lived his early years in the house on the left corner. It is now the office of a cooperative.
(James Brockman, S.J.)

younger sister Zaida and his younger brother Tiberio vividly remember their childhood days and their mother's suffering:

We scraped by. Mother had to rent out the upper part of the house, so the laundry area got moved to the down-stairs patio where there was no roof. When it rained, everything got soaked. She got wet one too many times working there. Her body started to go into paralysis, and she ended up crippled. And to top it all off the tenants were these cheapskates that didn't even pay! We had bad luck because our father also lost some coffee lands to an unscrupulous moneylender. So we barely managed to put food on the table for everyone.[29]

Elderly townspeople remember Romero as a serious child, studious and pious. Not much is known about a serious illness he suffered as a child. He went to public school for the first three years and later studied under a local tutor, Anita Iglesias, until he was twelve or thirteen. During that time, he was apprenticed to his father first as a letter carrier, and later as a telegraph operator.

*"God enters the human heart by its own ways. He enters the wise through wisdom. He enters the simple through simplicity."*
—November 25, 1977

A souvenir of Oscar's first trip to San Salvador, 1928. (Elvira Chacón)

His father taught him to play the bamboo flute and to read music, and he later learned to play the piano and harmonium in the seminary. Romero loved music, especially marimba music, a love he carried with him throughout his life.

His father, however, did not want Romero to continue his studies but to learn a trade. He was apprenticed by his father to one of the local carpenters, where he learned to make doors and tables, and he always stopped at one of the town's two churches on his way home from work:

> Of all of us, he was probably the one who prayed the most. Our father, Santos, had him apprenticed to Juan Leiva, the best carpenter in Ciudad Barrios, so Oscar worked alongside him and made doors, tables, china cabinets and even coffins. But more than anything else, he prayed. "I never saw a kid pray so much," Leiva would say. Because Oscar would go running out after his time in the carpentry shop and go straight to church for his prayers. Who knows? Maybe some day they'll make a national monument out of that place where he used to pray as a kid. And at night, he'd jump out of the bed he shared with Mamerto to kneel on the floor and say a few more prayers, wouldn't he? That destiny given by God was already a part of him.[30]

While many Salvadoran families were very devout, it was unusual that they would ever dream of being able to send a son to study for the priesthood. Most children never had the opportunity or the means to even consider such a vocation. At least

*"How beautiful will be the day when all the baptized understand that their work, their job, is a priestly work, that just as I celebrate Mass at this altar, so each carpenter celebrates Mass at his workbench."*

—November 20, 1977

As a boy Oscar was apprenticed to work in this carpentry shop.
(James Brockman, S.J.)

Romero, third from left, in the minor seminary of San Miguel, 1930. (Zoila Aurora Asturias and Eva del Carmen Asturias)

that was his father's belief, and for that reason, he sent his son to learn a trade. When Romero was thirteen, however, he expressed his desire to go to the seminary to the vicar general of the San Miguel diocese on one of his trips to Ciudad Barrios.

Years later, recalling his desire to become a priest, one of his friends recounted this story:

Ciudad Barrios awoke from its peasant slumber as soon as the sun raised its head above the horizon in the usual place . . . Guadalupe de Jesús got the new clothes ready so her son would be neat and presentable. So the boy went about, here, there and everywhere, accompanying the bishop on all his rounds. The bishop was quite impressed with him . . .

"Oscar, come over here!" the bishop called to him in front of his townspeople.

"Yes, Monseñor?"

"Tell me, boy, what do you want to be when you grow up?"

"Well, I . . . I would like to be a priest!"

Then the bishop raised his hefty finger and pointed it straight at Oscar's forehead. "You are going to be a bishop."

After marking the destiny of the boy, he went back to

Romero in the third row with his classmates. The minor seminary in San Miguel was directed by Claretian priests. (Zoila Aurora Asturias and Eva del Carmen Asturias)

*"Your word is pardon and gentleness for the penitent, Your word is holy instruction, eternal teaching; It is light to brighten, advice to hearten; It is voice of help, fire that burns, Way, truth, sublime splendor, Life—eternity."*
—Poem written in the minor seminary

his mansion in San Miguel. And Ciudad Barrios went back to its drowsy sleep.

Fifty years later, Monseñor Romero touched that place on his forehead and told me, "I can still feel the touch of his finger right here."[31]

In 1930, at age thirteen, he left home for the minor seminary in San Miguel run by the Claretians, seven hours on horseback from Ciudad Barrios. But he kept his ties with his family, sending his laundry home with a family friend and returning home for vacations.

When his mother became ill after the birth of her eighth child, and the family could not afford medicines, Oscar interrupted his studies to return home and help his family. He went to work for three months with his oldest brother Gustavo in the Potosi gold mine, a few miles from Ciudad Barrios, before returning to the seminary.

He remembered his years in the minor seminary fondly and wrote about how the seminarians lived together with the Claretian priests as one family. In 1937, at age twenty, Romero left the minor seminary in San Miguel to study theology at the national seminary in San Salvador run by the Jesuits.

# How Sad Is the Evening!

Not much is known about Santos Romero, Romero's father. What we do know is that Oscar Romero remembered his father with affection, and wrote movingly of his father's death in 1937:

*The sun goes slowly to its setting, the afternoon grows languid. His eyelids, drooping sadly, are robbing the day of its splendor, its joy, its light. How sad is the evening! . . .*

*Everything, my God, speaks of sadness, of weeping. But, oh, within my breast today is an eventide more sorrowful. My gaze, lost beyond the distant peaks of the east, looks for comfort; but the east, my unforgettable east, has become for me a setting sun. My father is dead!*

*Dear Father, I who each evening turned my gaze to the distant east, sending you my loving distant thought, would think of you on the porch of the home I remembered . . . would see you turning your gaze to the west where your son was . . .*

*Only the memories remain, memories of childhood—how you would pace the bedroom floor as my child's understanding memorized the Our Father, the Hail Mary, the Creed, the Hail Holy Queen, the commandments that your fatherly lips taught me . . .*

*I still see you one night waiting for us to return with Mother from our trip to San Miguel, waiting with a toy for each of us made with your own hands.*[32]

Zoila Aurora Asturias and Eva del Carmen Asturias

# Seminary

*"As Pope Pius XI explained when he decreed the feast of Christ the King, that does not mean that Christ is isolated from the power and wealth of earth. It means that he will use a different basis, a religious basis, to judge the consciences of political leaders and of the rich . . . from the eschatological and transcendent perspective of God's reign."*

—January 14, 1979

Soon after his father's death, Romero left to finish his studies under Jesuit professors at the Gregorian University in Rome. Pius XI was pope when Romero arrived, and he soon admired him for his opposition to fascism. "This is the pope I most admire."[33] Years later, on his final trip to Rome in 1980, Romero visited Pius XI's tomb and recalled with affection Pius' words: "While I am pope, no one will laugh at the church."[34]

One of Romero's friends and fellow students recalls his serious demeanor at the time:

> He had a deliberate bearing, like one who is not hurried to arrive because he knows he will get there. With other persons he was peaceable, calm—like one who knows that life has to be taken as it comes—rather quiet, a bit shy. His conduct was irreproachable; I never knew of anything that would lessen this judgment. He was observant of the regulations, pious, concerned for his priestly training in every aspect. With others, he could make friends and was regarded by us who were his friends for his simplicity and desire to help.[35]

Traveling to Rome on board the Orazio, 1937.
(Zoila Aurora Asturias and Eva del Carmen Asturias)

In September 1939, war broke out with the Nazi invasion of Poland and engulfed all of Europe in a wave of destruction that lasted until May 1945. Romero later described the suffering of those years:

*Europe and almost the whole world were a conflagration during the Second World War. Fear, uncertainty, news of bloodshed made for an environment of dread. At the Latin American College, rations grew smaller by the day. Father Rector would go out looking for something to eat and return with squashes, onions, chestnuts, whatever he could find, under his cloak. Hunger forced several Italian seminaries to close. The Latin American College had to cope with the situation, since all of its students were foreigners away from home; those who could return to their homelands took their chances in doing so. Almost every night sirens warned of enemy planes and one had to run for the shelters; twice they were more than an alarm and Rome's outskirts were scarred by horrible bombings.*[36]

In 1940, when Romero was twenty-two years old, he published an article in the student magazine of the Latin American College in Rome, in which he shared his view of the priesthood.

*This is your heritage, O priest: the cross. And this is your mission: to portion out the cross. Bearer of pardon and peace, the priest runs to the bed of the dying, and a cross in his hand is the key that opens the heavens and closes the abyss . . . To be a priest means to be, with Christ, a crucified one who redeems and to be, with Christ, a risen one who apportions resurrection and life.*[37]

Romero received his licentiate degree in theology *cum laude* in 1941, but he had to wait another year before he could be ordained because he was younger than the required age. On April 4, 1942, at age twenty-four, Romero was ordained a priest in Rome.

Romero subsequently began a doctoral dissertation on ascetical theology and Christian perfection according to Luis de la Puente, a sixteenth-century Spanish ascetical writer. While working on his dissertation, he wrote, "In recent days . . . the Lord has inspired in me a great desire for holiness. I've been thinking of how far a soul can ascend if it lets itself be possessed entirely by God."[38] But before he could finish his dissertation, his bishop summoned him to El Salvador.

Sixty years later, Monseñor Jesús Delgado, one of Romero's

In the Vatican with Pope Pius XII. Romero is to the right of the pope.
(Zoila Aurora Asturias and Eva del Carmen Asturias)

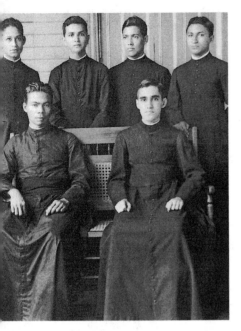

With fellow seminary students.
(Zoila Aurora Asturias and Eva del Carmen Asturias )

*"The Lord has inspired in me a great desire for holiness. I've been thinking of how far a soul can ascend if it lets itself be possessed entirely by God."*

friends and his first biographer, discovered pages of a diary Romero kept while he was a student in Rome.[39] The pages reveal a timid, but generous soul, with a solitary and mystical bent, marked by a profound devotion to the Sacred Heart of Jesus and a deep desire for sanctity.

The young Romero of his student years in Rome knew who he was. He knew, like St. Paul, his weakness. He was a timid person. But like St. Paul, too, he believed in the strength that comes from Christ when we allow him to live in us. "I live, but not I, rather Christ lives in me" (Galatians 2:19). "I can do all things in Him who comforts me" (Philippians 4:13).

Drawn forward by a profound mystical vocation, Romero was from his youth a person of Christ-centered faith. He loved the church profoundly, a love he discovered above all as a bishop. His love for the pope was noteworthy. With time, he discovered the church as the people of God that walks through history toward its eschatological consummation.

His youthful aspirations to sanctity he kept during his years of maturing into an adult. God our Father confirmed his priestly sanctity allowing him to die at the altar, when he offered the fruits of the earth and the work of human hands. Before Romero, Jesus had consummated this sacrifice. Monseñor Romero ended his life adoring Jesus in heaven.[40]

In August 1943, Romero and his lifelong friend from seminary days, Rafael Valladares, boarded a ship bound for Spain and Cuba. Upon arrival in Cuba, they were promptly arrested by Cuban police and placed in an internment camp, perhaps because they had come from Italy, one of the Axis powers.

However, they were soon released with the help of Redemptorist priests in Havana and continued on to Mexico, where they disembarked and traveled over land to El Salvador, arriving in San Miguel just in time for Christmas.

# Parish Priest

Romero offered his first solemn Mass in his hometown, Ciudad Barrios, on January 11, 1944. The souvenir card from that Mass reads: "May this sacrifice that we offer please you, O Lord. Govern with constant protection your servant, the Roman Pontiff. —Oscar A. Romero—my first solemn Mass, Ciudad Barrios, January 11, 1944."[41]

Years later, one of those present, though just a child at the time, recalled the celebration:

Celebrating the Eucharist, El Cuco Beach, San Miguel, 1948.
(Zoila Aurora Asturias and Eva del Carmen Asturias)

I was walking one day to visit my grandmother who lived in Morazan. I was a vagabond of a kid—only 10 years old—but already I liked to go all over getting to know new places. I arrived and saw that Ciudad Barrios was all decorated up with coffee flowers and paper flags, and that they'd even brought in a marimba band. "Hmmm," I thought, "maybe I'll stay."

"A priest from here is going to say his first Mass in this church." Everyone knew about it except me, since I wasn't from there. But when I found out, I went into the church to check it out and see everything from beginning to end with my own eyes . . .

I arrived at my grandmother's house pretty late at night, all disheveled. She was one of these really religious women.

"Why are you coming in so late, young man?"

"I was at the Mass celebrated by a new priest."

"What priest . . . ?

I gave my grandmother the little prayer card they'd given out during the Mass. I couldn't read it, but his name was written there: Oscar Arnulfo Romero. First Solemn Mass. Ciudad Barrios, January 11, 1944.

"I have a feeling that priest is going to be a bishop," I told her.

"Oh, so you're a fortune-teller, are you? What do you know about being a bishop?"

"I don't know about it, but I can imagine."[42]

*"One day, there will be no more Masses, no more need of temporal priests, because all of us, through the labors of priests, of bishops, of catechists, of lay ministers of the word, of all God's priestly people, will have achieved humanity's incorporation into Christ and Christ will be the one priest . . ."*
—December 10, 1977

Zoilz Aurora Asturias and Eva del Carmen Asturias

Romero was initially assigned by his bishop to a small mountain parish in Anamoros, a town in the neighboring department of La Union. The bishop, however, soon called him to serve as his diocesan secretary in San Miguel, a town of about twenty thousand people, where he remained for the next twenty-three years.

Romero became the pastor of the cathedral parish, and chaplain of San Francisco, a little church where the venerated image of Our Lady of Peace was kept until the cathedral was ready to house it. He began his pastoral assignment with great zeal, organizing catechism classes and first communions, visiting the rural areas and the city jails, and working with the diocesan radio and the newspaper.[43]

Prayer and meditation were part of Romero's daily routine, and each evening he organized a holy hour before the Blessed Sacrament, praying the rosary with the people and preaching. He was known as a good preacher, and people who remember his sermons remember that he insisted that religion deal with daily life and not mere piety.

In 1954, Romero undertook the month-long Spiritual Exercises of St. Ignatius Loyola. Throughout his life, he continued to rely on the Jesuits for spiritual direction and confession. When he became a bishop, he took a phrase from the spiritual exercises, *Sentir con la Iglesia*—"to be of one mind and heart with the Church"—as his episcopal motto.[44]

People who knew Romero at this time remember him as a caring pastor, hard-working and very devout.

He was on the go at all hours of the day and night. Hearing confessions the whole blessed day or the whole never-ending night after a rosary. That takes patience, now that I think about it! It was a constant effort because in San Francisco there was a rosary every night. He never wasted an opportunity! One day—he told us sacristans— he was almost finished hearing confessions when . . .

"Father, what penance should I do?" a woman asked him.

"You should pray five pesos," he mumbled.

He had fallen asleep! That's the way he was. He would work without stopping, until he was totally burned out.[45]

Father Romero was a friend to rich and poor alike. His concern for the poor was genuine, a concern that may be traced back to his own experience of hardship and poverty in his younger years. Just as he was known for his piety, so too was he known for his charity, as several people testify:

> The drunks were the ones who sought him out the most . . . We saw his patience with my brother Angelito. If Romero were there when Angelito came home after a big drinking spree, he wouldn't let any of us reproach him or hassle him.
>
> "Come here, Angelito," he would say, "Sit down next to me and play the flute for me."
>
> So he'd play Mexican and Guatemalan folk songs, which he could do really nicely, and the music would calm Angelito down. So you see, Father Romero always had a soft spot for drunks and for the downtrodden in life.[46]

Zoila Aurora Asturias and Eva del Carmen Asturias

> The big coffee plantation owners of San Miguel were very close to him. They'd give him money for charity and invite him to their farms, and he'd celebrate special masses in their plantation homes or go at Christmas time and help them hand out little presents to the poor workers there. Everyone knew that.[47]

Romero, however, was not without his critics. Some saw such a charitable approach as a way of avoiding the underlying issues of justice and oppression:

> Romero was like St. Vincent de Paul—a mass of poor people always followed him around. Of course, with his way of thinking, he always got the rich people to pay alms so that he could give them to the poor. That way the poor could have some relief for their problems and the rich could relieve their consciences.[48]

*"Blessed are the poor, for they know that their riches are in the One who being rich made himself poor in order to enrich us with his poverty, teaching us the Christian's true wisdom."*
—January 29, 1978

# Sharing the Gospel

One person who was a beneficiary to Romero's charity was Alejandro Ortiz,[49] a poor campesino who was the father of Father Octavio Ortiz, the first priest ordained by Romero, and one who was also eventually assassinated.

In 1952, around Christmas time, I wove three hammocks that were each about eight feet long and I told my wife:

"I'm going to go to San Miguel to sell them, and with what I make, I'm going to buy a Bible."

. . . I went running to the church of San Francisco, and there I was allowed to see Father Romero.

"You know what? I don't have any Bibles here right now," he told me, "but I'm going to make a telephone call to San Salvador so they'll send me some on the afternoon truck. We'll have them by tomorrow, if you want to wait . . ."

"I'd be happy to wait, Father, but where would I stay the night?"

"No problem. You can do what you need to in the city, look around, and later on you can come back and sleep here in the convent."

I felt so welcomed even though I was just a poor campesino, a peasant farmer . . . When it was already late, I went back and I saw that other people were sleeping there too—other poor people. He had given them all a place.

My Bible had arrived in the afternoon so I finally had a way to read the stories first hand. As I was leaving, Father Romero gave me some advice.

"It's good to read the Bible by yourself, but it's even better if you read it together with other people. It's like when you go to gather nance fruits with a group. The more people that go, the more you pick up, and the better the harvest."

I went back home. And from then on I always listened to Father Romero on *Radio Chaparrastique*, where he was on every day talking about Bible passages.[50]

With children in San Miguel. (Zoila Aurora Asturias and Eva del Carmen Asturias)

Mirian Oseguda

Pastoral visits in San Miguel.

Romero loved the radio as a means of communication, and he would continue to offer catechetical programs on the radio throughout his life. Even as archbishop, the radio continued to be an effective means of communication to broadcast his weekly homilies, and thousands of people listened to them every week:

Courtesy Equipo Maíz

All of us in the eastern part of the country knew about him because of his programs on Radio Chaparrastique. I was a second grader in La Union, and I never missed an opportunity to listen to him.

*Laudetur Jesus Christus.* Those were the closing words of his much-listened-to Morning Prayer and Evening Prayer. I liked hearing those Latin words so much, I would recite them by memory. There were also some great programs on *El Padre Vicente*, where they would tell real-life stories. All those things I heard on the radio really opened my mind. I learned from them.

A lot of people would write him letters asking about certain topics, asking for advice or financial help, or volunteering for his charities. And he would read that whole mess of letters on the radio. I loved that program because there was so much participation.[51]

# His Mother's Hands

*"It moves one's heart to think: Nine months before I was born, there was a woman who loved me deeply. She did not know what I was going to be like, but she loved me because she carried me in her womb. And when she gave birth to me, she took me in her arms because her love was not just beginning —she conceived it along with me . . . God is the exquisite likeness of a mother with child."*

—July 30, 1978

Almost twenty years after Romero was assigned to the cathedral parish in San Miguel, his mother died. She and his younger brother had accompanied Romero to his new home in San Miguel from the beginning.

Doña Guadalupe de Jesús Galdámez, his mother, or Niña Jesús as we called her, died in 1961. She had lived near her son, Father Romero, since he'd been assigned his priestly duties here in San Miguel. By the time he got here, her arm was already paralyzed by disease, and there was practically no feeling left in it. She was very quiet.

Every week Father Romero would go to visit her in the neighborhood of San Francisco where she lived. You could look at her face and see that mother and son looked exactly alike. Her face was his face. Her hands were his hands. You could see that the way she gestured with her hand was the same way he moved his. Maybe his jaw was more pronounced than his mother's, but even that trait he got from her.[52]

Perhaps the clearest indication of how Romero's heart and compassion for the poor were shaped by his own experience of poverty is given in this anecdote about his mother's funeral:

She died, and we buried her in San Miguel. And since Father Romero had relationships with the upper-class families of San Miguel—from the Garcia Prietos on down—people from the aristocracy went to the funeral. Coffee plantation owners showed up, and even a famous pianist from there. But since he also had friends like us who loved him, we went too. Nuns went, and children went. His whole family also arrived in San Miguel on that sad occasion, and we saw what they were like—of humble bearing. On the way to the cemetery after the funeral Mass, who do you think he walked with? He didn't go with the upper crust; he walked alongside the ones in simple dress, in country clothes—us!

"I was born with them. I'll go with them," he said quietly. And that was what the whole way was like—him alongside the casket and alongside the crowds of the poor.[53]

Oscar with his mother Guadalupe, Ciudad Barrios, 1944. (Courtesy Zaida Romero)

# Winds of Change

Nineteen hundred thirty-two was a key year in Salvadoran history. That was the year of la matanza, when the Salvadoran military crushed a Communist-inspired peasant uprising, killing thirty thousand people. Ever since 1932, El Salvador had been ruled by a series of military dictators, until the 1980s.

Romero was fifteen years old and in the seminary when that repression took place. The church at that time was conservative, allied to wealthy landowners and to the military—as it was throughout Latin America. By the 1960s, however, everything was about to change.

The population of El Salvador quadrupled during Romero's lifetime, widening even more the gap between abject poverty and ostentatious wealth. The poor had become aware of their oppression, and political parties on the left had begun to organize movements for social justice and liberation. The military who ruled the country increased their repression against the poor.

Council Fathers assembled at Vatican II. (Courtesy Maryknoll Archives)

Zoila Aurora Asturias and Eva del Carmen Asturias

At the same time these changes were taking place in El Salvador, the ground for radical changes in the church was being prepared. In the 1950s the Jesuits founded the Central American University in San Salvador with a mission to educate the poor.

Foreign missionary priests—including Basque Jesuits, Irish Franciscans, Spanish Dominicans and Passionists, and Flemish priests from the diocese of Bruges—and many religious orders of women, were involved in the promotion of lay movements in the church, based on the Catholic Action formula of "See— Judge—Act." Lay catechists and basic Christian communities were formed, and the Bible was placed in the hands of the poor and read from the perspective of their social reality and in the light of the Gospel.

From 1962 to 1965, the Second Vatican Council ushered in a renewal of the church. Romero was aware of these changes, but he saw the council largely as a call to priestly renewal. He had always been a devout priest, read Pope John XXIII's *Journal of a Soul* with interest, and noted that the pope also practiced the same Ignatian Spiritual Exercises and devotions that he did.[54]

Shortly before celebrating his silver anniversary as a priest on April 4, 1967, Romero received the title of Monseñor. But his uncompromising attitudes and traditional ways had created resentment in the diocesan clergy in San Miguel, to the point they had even asked the bishop to remove him from the offices that he held in the diocese.[55]

A few months later, Romero was named Secretary-General of the Salvadoran Bishops' Conference and on September 1, 1967, he celebrated his last Mass as pastor of the cathedral parish in San Miguel and left to take up residence in San Salvador. Not everybody was sorry to see Romero go:

We thought he would be the new bishop of San Miguel. Pretty much everyone thought so. Who would it be if it weren't Father Romero? He was the priest that everyone knew, the one in charge of everything. He'd be the one to be named, right? But he wasn't made a bishop, and they didn't let him stay in San Miguel either. We never knew why, just that he'd received an order instructing him to go to San Salvador to work as a secretary for all the rest of the bishops.

There was a going-away party for him at the movie theater in San Miguel. A huge crowd arrived and they couldn't even all fit inside. Rich, poor, kind-of-rich, kind-of-poor—we all showed up at the gathering. Everybody was there! . . .

Do you want me to be frank? Father Romero? He was a friend of the poor and a friend of the rich. To the rich he would say, "Love the poor." And to us poor he would tell us to love God, and that God knew what He was doing by putting us last in line, and that afterwards we would be assured a place in heaven. He would preach to us about the heaven where rich people who gave alms would go and where poor people who didn't cause too much trouble would go . . .

Father Romero? He went around with sheep and with wolves, and his thinking was that the sheep and the wolves should eat from the same dish, because that's what was pleasing to God . . . Everyone applauded and burst into tears because after 23 years he was leaving San Miguel. But as for me personally, I can't say I was too sorry to see him go.[56]

# Medellín

Upon his arrival in San Salvador in September 1967, Romero took up residence at San José la Montaña, the major seminary of the bishops. The Jesuits had run the seminary since 1915, but tensions with the Jesuits resulted in the bishops taking back control of the seminary in 1972, preferring a more conservative approach to the training of priests.

In addition to his duties with the national conference of bishops, Romero also became secretary of the Central American Bishops' Conference. One of the seminary students at the time recalls seeing the light on in his room until very late at night.

When he arrived in San Salvador, preparations were already underway for the Latin American bishops' meeting in Medellín—the meeting that shook the whole Church to its core . . .

His way of thinking was very different from the one that was brewing in Latin America, but as far as paperwork and documents were concerned, he put all of his effort into getting things just right. When all was said and done, it was still the work of the Church, and in those matters, he was a perfectionist.

The winds of Medellín were already beginning to blow, and many of the bishops had stopped wearing their long black cassocks. But him? Forget it. He kept wearing his. One day on the way back from one of those bishops' meetings, he told us seminarians as if he were embarrassed, "You wouldn't believe how out of place I felt. I was the only one in the whole room wearing black!"[57]

In 1968, the Conference of Latin American Bishops (CELAM) met for the second time in ten years, this time in Medellín, Colombia. In the words of Penny Lernoux, author of *Cry of the People,* "Medellín produced the Magna Carta of today's persecuted, socially committed Church and, as such, rates as one

*"A deafening cry pours from the throats of millions of men and women, asking their pastors for a liberation that reaches them from nowhere else . . . The poverty of the Church and of its members in Latin America ought to be a sign and a commitment—a sign of the inestimable value of the poor in the eyes of God, an obligation of solidarity with those who suffer."*

—Medellín documents

The major seminary of the bishops in San Salvador, where Romero lived in 1967. (James Brockman, S.J.)

of the major political events of the century: it shattered the centuries-old alliance of Church, military and the rich elites."[58]

Two key words emerged at Medellín: liberation and participation. According to the bishops, the mass of people in Latin America were oppressed by the "institutionalized violence" of the dominant social, economic, and political structures. Liberation was understood "in the biblical sense of physical and spiritual salvation, the Exodus of the Old Testament and the Good News promised by Christ in his first public pronouncement."[59]

Participation referred to the work of Brazilian educator Paulo Freire, and his work of "conscientization," or consciousness-raising. As Lernoux writes, "The aim was to make people aware of themselves and their environment, to learn to think. And once people begin to think, they ask questions. They want to know why their village has no running water, for example, and what they can do about it. That is the seed of civic participation, making Latin Americans reflective agents for change."[60]

Closely related to liberation and participation was the formation of basic Christian communities as a medium for evangelization. Lernoux writes, "Unlike parish structures that encompass a heterogeneous population with different outlooks and lifestyles, Christian communities are small (on average, twelve to fifteen members), tightly knit groups of people with similar incomes, jobs, education, problems, and aspirations . . . Because their orientation is a liberating one based on the techniques of consciousness-raising, particularly the reading of the Bible, these groups develop a dynamic of their own. They soon add appendages such as schools, cooperatives, and health units."[61]

Within three years, these three goals—liberation, participation, and basic Christian communities—had taken root in El Salvador. Romero, however, had grown uneasy with the changes in the church, particularly those produced by Medellín.

Salvador Carranza, one of the Jesuits who lived with Romero at the major seminary said of Romero at the time:

We never saw him attend anything that resembled a pastoral activity. He didn't have a parish. And he didn't go to the clergy meetings. If he did go, he would hide in some corner and never open his mouth. He was afraid of confronting the more active priests who were being radical-

*"We, the bishops, wish to come closer to the poor in sincerity and brotherhood, making ourselves accessible to them. We ought to sharpen the awareness of our duty of solidarity with the poor, to which charity leads us. This solidarity means that we make ours their problems and their struggles, that we know how to speak with them. This has to be concretized in criticism of injustice and oppression, in the struggles against the intolerable situation which a poor person often has to tolerate, in the willingness to dialogue with the groups responsible for that situation in order to make them understand their obligations."*

—Medellín documents

ized by everything that was happening in the country—
and there was a lot happening! But he preferred to stay in
his office buried in his papers. Or to walk down the halls
dressed in his black cassock praying the breviary.

Soon after he arrived in San Salvador, we had a Pastoral
Week that was a real shaker-upper! Everything went into
high gear and became more radical. Plans, meetings, formation of communities—a thousand things were getting
underway! He stayed on the margins of all of that. Later
he started to take sides, but against us. People were talking
about his psychological problems back then. They said he
took trips to Mexico to recover. It was also said that he was
close to some of the Opus Dei priests here in San Salvador.
He had his world, and it was not like ours. He started off
on the wrong foot from the very beginning.[62]

On April 21, 1970, Romero
received a call from the nuncio
that the current archbishop of
San Salvador, Luis Chávez y
González, had asked him to
name Romero as auxiliary bishop. His episcopal ordination
took place on June 21. The
president of El Salvador, Fidel
Sánchez Hernández, as well as
all the bishops of El Salvador,
attended. Rutilio Grande, SJ,
served as master of ceremonies.

Not everyone was happy
that Romero had been named a
bishop. His ways seemed wed-
ded to the past, and the lavish
ceremony seemed in contradiction to the dire poverty in
which the majority of people in El Salvador lived. Romero was
out of step with the hopes that many of the diocesan clergy held
out for the church since Medellín.

Romero's episcopal consecration.
On the right is Father Rutilio
Grande, who served as master of
ceremonies for the celebration.
(Courtesy Publicaciónes Pastorales del
Arzobispado)

# The National Pastoral Week

On June 22, 1970, the day after Romero's episcopal ordination, the National Pastoral Week was organized by Archbishop Chávez and his auxiliary bishop Arturo Rivera y Damas to introduce Vatican II and Medellín into the archdiocese. One hundred and twenty-three priests, men and women religious, and lay people participated in the week.

> The new pastoral methods coming into use in those years furthered the training of lay leaders, catechists, and delegates of the Word (lay persons delegated by the community to lead Bible discussions and prayer services), as well as the formation of communities among campesinos. Bible study and a communitarian approach to the sacraments figured prominently . . .
>
> The basic ideas of liberation theology were already current in such gatherings in Latin America and were also embedded in the Medellín documents: that God does not will social injustice, but rather the opposite, and that people must work and struggle with God's help to bring about justice. Such ideas immediately challenge the social order and those in power and lead to political conflict. To a person schooled in a vision of life in which one must accept suffering and seek peace and harmony at any price, such ideas involve a considerable readjustment of attitudes and preconceptions.[63]

Meanwhile, tensions within the country had already begun to boil over. In 1969, the expulsion by Honduras of tens of thousands of Salvadoran peasants during the "soccer war" accentuated social and political tensions in El Salvador over land.[64] Teachers and peasants both pressed the government for change, and encountered further repression.

Bishop Romero continued to view the changes in the church as partially responsible for these conflicts. The source of many of these tensions, according to Romero, could be found in the liberating orientation of the Jesuits.

In 1971, when Romero was named editor of *Orientación*, the archdiocesan newspaper, he immediately began to pen articles criticizing the Jesuits for "false liberating education." The following year, the Jesuits were expelled from the major seminary by the bishops, and Romero was named the new rector. Francisco Estrada, SJ, writes:

View of cathedral of San Salvador.
(Octavio Duran)

> At the time, I was the Jesuit Provincial, and I went to talk to Monseñor Romero directly.
>
> "Look," I told him rather angrily, "You're accusing us of very serious things and I want you to tell me what you're basing these accusations on. Because the authority that I recognize—the only authority I recognize—is Archbishop Chávez, and he knows exactly what's being taught in our school. We've never taken a single step without his approval . . ." He didn't even look at me. I discovered that even though he waged heated battles, he was really a timid man.
>
> "I want to know what you are basing these accusations on!
>
> "What reliable sources could you possibly have? In the case of the school, the only sources are me, the Provincial of the Society of Jesus, and the Archbishop of San Salvador, of whom you are simply an auxiliary! What other source could you possibly have to be causing such an uproar? Tell me!"
>
> He didn't look up.
>
> "I have reliable sources of information." He didn't change his words or his tone.
>
> But I've already told you who the only reliable sources are! What are these sources of yours?"
>
> "I have reliable sources."
>
> That man drove me totally crazy. He didn't give me a single argument or a single reason. He didn't dialogue. He didn't ask me questions. He didn't want to know.[65]

Hopes for a major political change in El Salvador were crushed when the military perpetrated major electoral fraud by installing its candidate despite his having lost the 1972

With fellow bishops. (Courtesy Equipo Maíz)

presidential elections. A coalition of Christian Democrats, Social Democrats, and Communists defeated the military's candidate, Colonel Arturo Armando Molina, but the military prevented the coalition from taking power. People rose up in protest in San Salvador, and the military decreed a state of siege, a curfew, and martial law throughout the country.

Colonel Molina started his presidency on July 1, 1972. On July 19, he ordered the invasion of the National University. There was a lot of violence and destruction. People were beaten with rifle butts, and about 800 were hauled off to jail. Starting then, the university was closed for a whole year. That was when things really heated up in San Salvador.

But, what do you know! The Bishops' Conference published a paid ad in the newspapers, written and signed by Monseñor Romero as Secretary, defending the occupation of the university with a rationalization taken straight from the government's statement: that the uni-

versity was a hotbed of subversion, and that it was necessary to take measures against it.[66]

The seeds of unrest had been sown, and these tensions would
explode into a full-blown civil war in less than a decade. Conflicts
began to spill over into other sectors of the church, and again
Bishop Romero was at the heart of the controversy. Zacamil,[67] one
of the first parishes to form basic Christian communities in San
Salvador, invited Bishop Romero to dialogue with the community:

We decided to invite Romero to celebrate Mass with the
Christian base communities in the neighborhood of
Zacamil. When he accepted—because he never said no to
a Mass—we made our true intentions known.

"We'll expect you then and, just so you know, we want
to reflect together in this Mass on what happened at the
university . . ."

His face changed colors, but he didn't back down . . .

"Monseñor, how can you believe the government
more than your people, more than us, your Church?" the
young men insisted.

"How can you believe a government that came to
power through fraud?"

"Fraud?! What kind of political judgments are
these?" he said, angrily. "Now I realize that you're not
doing pastoral work here at all. You're doing political
work! And you haven't called me to a Mass. You've called
me to a meeting of subversives!"

By then he had totally lost his cool.

"Look, Monseñor, in this environment of distrust,
even though we're all part of the same Church, we don't
have the conditions necessary to be able to celebrate Mass
. . . So let's call it off. The Mass is over!" . . .

He left. No one went with him, or paid him any attention. The people were angry at first, then embarrassed,
and then for a long time, they were just totally confused.

There has never been such a harsh confrontation with
Monseñor Romero in any community in San Salvador as
we had there that day in Zacamil.[68]

*"As the magi from the East
followed their star and found
Jesus, who filled their hearts
with boundless joy, let us too,
even in hours of uncertainty, of
shadows, of darkness, like those
the magi had, not fail to follow
that star, the star of our faith."*
—January 8, 1978

# Bishop of Santiago de María

These tensions in the Archdiocese of San Salvador were relieved somewhat when Romero was named Bishop of the Diocese of Santiago de María on October 15, 1974. The diocese included Romero's hometown, Ciudad Barrios, and stretched across the two departments of San Miguel and Usulután.

With this new appointment, Romero felt vindicated for the stands that he had taken with respect to the Jesuits and the basic Christian communities in El Salvador. In a parting editorial in the archdiocesan newspaper, *Orientación*, he wrote:

*This trust of the pope in its editor must also be interpreted as the most solemn backing of the church's magisterium for the ideology that has inspired the paper's pages under this editorship. This silent approval from so high a source constitutes the best reward and satisfaction for all of us who work together for this ideal, at the same time that it determines the route to follow.*[69]

Subsequently, he went to Rome to thank Pope Paul VI for naming him a bishop. For Romero, his trip to Rome "had the same meaning as St. Paul's historic trip to Jerusalem to see Peter and to check his criteria against those of the See that is the center of Catholic unity and guarantee of the church's authentic teaching."[70]

On December 14, 1974, Romero was installed as Bishop of the Diocese of Santiago de María in a festive celebration attended by government and church officials alike. For Romero, however, many things would soon change. Already, the seeds of Romero's conversion were taking root.

According to Father Juan Macho, the Passionist priest who was his pastoral vicar, Romero often quoted Vatican II, but never Medellín, in his homilies.[71] He still had his doubts about the radical changes taking place among the Salvadoran peasants, who were becoming aware of their oppression and beginning to organize themselves at catechetical training centers like Los Naranjos, run by the Passionist priests.

"The teaching you do is too participatory." That's what

Monseñor Romero would say most often when we would talk about the work at Los Naranjos Center. He had finally let us open it again. Sometimes he would come at me with another kind of argument:

"I've heard it said that the government is worried about this type of teaching, too."

"The government? But who should tell me what the correct teaching is? The government or my bishop? Because if it's the government, then I have no use for you. But if it's you, then I don't care what the government says!"

You just couldn't tell about him. He couldn't just take a stand and move on it. From the very beginning, any time that I or anyone else mentioned Medellín to him, the man would get so nervous, he'd develop a tic. The corner of his lip would start trembling. It would shake and shake, and he couldn't control it. Really, hearing about Medellín and having his lip tremble were one and the same thing.

But still, he was learning. Learning from reality.[72]

Romero at his consecration as bishop, San Miguel, July 29, 1970. (Zoila Aurora Asturias and Eva del Carmen Asturias)

And Romero still had his doubts about the radical changes taking place in the church. On July 12, 1975, he wrote a letter to Pope Paul VI, supporting the beatification of the founder of the archconservative organization Opus Dei and expressing gratitude for the priests who up until that time had served as his spiritual directors. He would maintain these contacts with Opus Dei until his death, despite his conversion.

On July 30, 1975, when the Salvadoran military killed forty university students in San Salvador, many priests and religious joined protesting students when they occupied the San Salvador cathedral. Romero, however, protested the occupation of churches as a form of protest.

The following year, Romero was named to the Pontifical Commission in Latin America and traveled to Rome to deliver a memorandum he wrote on the "political theology" of the Jesuits, the "socio-political" orientation of the Inter-Diocesan Justice and Peace Commission, and the "political involvement" of priests in the catechetical training centers run by the church, including Los Naranjos.

On August 6, 1976, the feast of the Transfiguration, Romero

preached the homily at the cathedral in San Salvador, decrying the "so-called new Christologies," an allusion, no doubt, to Jesuit theologian Jon Sobrino's book *Christology at the Crossroads.*[73]

All these incidents reveal a more cautious, conservative bent in Romero's approach to pastoral ministry. Still, glimpses of Romero's compassion for the poor and his concern for justice could be seen in his pastoral visits on horseback to peasant families to learn about their reality.

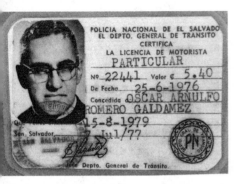

Romero's driver's license. (Octavio Duran)

Santiago de María is a thousand meters above sea level. The harvest months are cold, and at night, it's really freezing. His first year, Romero didn't notice. But during the second year, he started realizing that the campesinos that arrived to work the coffee harvest on the plantations were sleeping on the sidewalks, scattered around the plaza, shivering with cold.

"What can be done?" he asked one day.

"Monseñor, you can solve the problem. Look at that big old house where the school used to be. Open it up!"

He opened it. Three hundred people could fit inside. He also opened a little classroom where we used to have our clergy meetings. Another 30 could sleep in there. And that's how he started giving shelter to a lot of people.

"And serve them something hot at night—a glass of hot corn atol or milk." He gave that order to the people that worked in Caritas.

While the campesinos were having their drink and getting warmed up, Romero would go around and talk with them. He spent a lot of time listening. That's how he began to understand that the problems we'd told him about so often were not stories that we'd made up.[74]

On November 28, 1976, just three months before he was named Archbishop of San Salvador, Romero issued a pastoral letter denouncing the treatment of the farmworkers who harvested coffee in his diocese. He cited the Scripture passage: "Behold, the day wage of the laborers that cut your fields, defrauded by you, is crying out, and the cries of the reapers have reached the ears of the Lord of hosts" (James 5:4).[75]

# Seeds of Conversion

Romero was bishop of Santiago de María for two years and two months. One of the reassessments of recent times is to refer back to this period as the beginning of his "conversion" to a faith committed to justice for the poor. Some testimonies refer to his own experience of poverty in his youth, and his pastoral concern for the poor as a parish priest in San Miguel, as evidence that such a conversion was ongoing throughout his life. His time in Santiago de María, however, was crucial to this journey.

Two of the Passionist priests who worked with Romero during this period give three reasons why Romero's time in the diocese provided a crucial foundation for the dramatic reality he would soon face as archbishop of San Salvador.[76]

Octavio Duran

First, after seven years of office work as Secretary to the Bishops' Conference of El Salvador, Romero returned to the direct pastoral activity with the people that had always characterized his ministry as a priest. Second, "a change began to take place in his ideas, both theological as well as pastoral . . . and in the way in which he looked at and judged reality." Finally, certain incidents that occurred while he was bishop of the diocese, particularly the massacre at Tres Calles, were important events in his deepening conversion and commitment to the poor.

During his three years as bishop in this largely rural diocese, Romero witnessed the growing conflict over land ownership. On November 29, 1974, these conflicts became more violent, and Salvadoran National Guardsmen killed six campesinos in La Cayetana, a village in the neighboring diocese of San Vicente. Seven months later, on June 21, 1975, units of the Salvadoran National Guard killed five peasants in Tres Calles, in Romero's own diocese.

The following day, Romero went to visit the families of the victims and offer Mass for their loved ones. During the Mass, he denounced the killings, calling them "a violation of human

*"Faith is what a child has when its father puts out his hands and says, 'Jump!' and the child leaps into space with the assurance that its father's hands won't let it fall."* —May 21, 1978

rights." Five days later he appealed to the president of El
Salvador in an anguished but deferential letter to protest the
killings, but he did not protest in public. He still believed it was
better to resolve problems quietly behind closed doors at the
level of church and civil authorities.

After writing President Molina, Romero sent a letter to his
fellow bishops explaining why he did not want to protest publicly. First, he thought it would be better to intervene as he had
done, directly with the military commander and the president;
second, he did not believe that the church was directly involved
in the affair; and third, he was not entirely aware of the motives
for the killings or what the conduct of the victims had been.[77]

This third reason was received with disillusionment by the
campesinos who heard his memorial Mass for the victims of the
massacre.

> Romero celebrated the ninth day memorial Mass for the
> dead at Tres Calles. That's where I met him. That
> Monseñor Romero made me mad. He was so wishy-
> washy! He talked about "the dead" instead of the people
> who had been "murdered" and he preached a sermon
> condemning violence, which practically suggested that
> those poor men had been killed because they were vio-
> lent, that they somehow had it coming to them. I remem-
> ber we had gone with a truckload of campesinos from
> Aguilares, all people who were participating in grassroots
> organizations. They went back from that Mass disillu-
> sioned.[78]

Pedro Ferradas, a Passionist priest who accompanied
Romero on that day to visit the bereaved families, shared this
testimony:

> The sun was coming up when I saw Monseñor Romero
> arrive. He already knew.
> "Father, let's go to Tres Calles!"
> We were too late to see the bodies. By the time we got
> to the village, they'd already been buried, and the people
> could only tell us how they'd found them—mutilated,
> tortured almost beyond recognition. The mother was

crying, the wives, the little children. We went inside their little houses. The boards still held the stench of blood. In the years to come we would become accustomed to these cruelties, but back then we were new to it. We spent almost three hours there, but our words failed us.

"They were strong, healthy men . . . Now look what's happened to them."

Monseñor Romero didn't say anything. He just listened to everything, and watched everything. As we were about to leave the village, we saw a group of campesinos off in the distance. We approached them. They'd found the body of another one of the people they'd been looking for. It had been thrown in a dry ditch that ran alongside of the road. He was just a kid, at the bottom of the ditch, face up. You could see the bullet holes, the bruises left by the blows, the dried blood. His eyes were open, as if asking the reason for his death and not understanding. One of the men took off his shirt to cover him. He was practically naked. They had the wake for him there, all of them with their machetes drawn. It wasn't grief they felt right then. It was rage.

Octavio Duran

Monseñor Romero mingled with all of them and prayed a slow responsorial prayer. He didn't say anything else. When we said good-bye and walked toward the road, the campesinos were all standing there still, immobile with their machetes and knives ready, sharpened. I broke the silence as we walked slowly away.

"Monseñor, it seems to me that if there aren't some changes in El Salvador, violence is going to break out all over—like water bursting a dam."

He didn't answer me. Eight well-armed National Guardsmen were coming towards us on the road toward the village. I could see that Monseñor Romero was frightened by the sight of them, but he didn't say anything. Fortunately, they didn't stop us. It wasn't until we were in the car on the way back that he finally spoke.

"Father Pedro, we have to find a way to evangelize the rich, so that they change, so that they convert!"

"Who knows, Monseñor . . . You know them. You have dealings with them. All of those rich families are

Octavio Duran

*"How it delights me in humble villages when the people come crowding around! Or you arrive at the town and they come out to meet you. They come with trust because they know that you are bringing them God's message."* —August 12, 1979

friends of yours. And they're the ones that order these kinds of killings . . . Who knows if they'll change."

We made the trip to Santiago in silence. The sun was setting, and I could imagine the light glinting off the blades of the machetes in Tres Calles.[79]

Less than two years later Romero would find himself again face to face with bereaving families, this time in the village of Aguilares as he gathered around the bodies of an old man, a young boy, and his friend, Father Rutilio Grande. The seeds of the conversion that took place that March night in Aguilares had already been sown two years earlier in Tres Calles.

# A Pastoral Experiment

Much of what had happened in El Salvador since the National Pastoral Week in 1970 was embodied in the pastoral work of Romero's close friend, Father Rutilio Grande, a Jesuit pastor of the rural parish of Aguilares, just north of the capital, San Salvador.[80]

In 1971, Rutilio Grande took a course at the Instituto Pastoral Latinamericano in Quito, Ecuador, in order to make contact with current thinking among Latin American theologians and pastoral workers.

While in Ecuador, he spent some time in Riobamba, the diocese of Bishop Leonidas Proaño, the great defender of the poor and of indigenous people, and later a candidate for the Nobel Peace Prize. There Grande learned the basic method of concientization, a method of consciousness-raising that he would later use in his evangelization work in Aguilares.

When he returned to El Salvador, Grande was named pastor of the parish of Aguilares, a microcosm of the social reality in El Salvador, where the best lands were occupied by sugar plantations, and the peasants subsisted on the worst lands and supplemented their own hard work with wage labor on the plantations. Grande's parish served the ten thousand people in the town, and another twenty thousand peasants in the surrounding rural areas.

From September 1972 until January 1973, Rutilio Grande headed a pastoral team of four Jesuits, several Jesuit seminarians, and university students from San Salvador who helped with the work. They divided the town and the rural areas into districts, and gave two-week "missions" centering on the work of evangelization. During the mission, the team would cover the entire area of the parish, deliberately eating each meal in a different house and listening to the problems of the people.

During the evening sessions, to which the whole community was invited, a Scripture passage was read, verse by verse, and interspersed with questions or comments. It was here that the information about the community gathered by the team was given back to the people after it had been analyzed and codified into basic images or key words, in the style of Paulo Freire. The team had a clear option to work within the framework of the people's religious vision. Their goal was to deepen and transform this vision from an attitude of passivity to one of active struggle for social change.

During this two-week period, a number of natural leaders began to emerge. The entire community participated in a process of selecting its own pastoral leaders, known as "Delegates of the Word." Emphasis was placed on a spirit of service and on collective leadership. As the two-week mission ended, the new delegates were presented to the community in a formal meeting.

This first phase of evangelization ended on Pentecost, 1973, with a Mass for everyone who had participated in the mission. Rutilio Grande reminded the people that their goal had been "a community of brothers and sisters, committed to building a new world according to God's plan, without oppressors or oppressed." As a result of this first phase, there were now ten urban basic Christian communities and twenty-seven rural ones, with three hundred pastoral leaders, or Delegates of the Word.

Since the early 1970s, peasants in El Salvador had begun to organize into cooperatives, such as FECCAS (Christian Federation of Peasants of El Salvador), and peasant unions, such as the UTC (Union of Rural Workers). These efforts were aimed at achieving better working conditions in the field and just wages for farmworkers. Such efforts were routinely met by cruel repression on the part of the landowners and military.

Many of the Delegates of the Word and members of the basic Christian communities of Aguilares became active in FECCAS. Questions were raised about the relation between political organizing and grassroots church work. Many on the pastoral team saw it as self-evident that the church should "accompany" the people in their search for effective ways to build grassroots organizations to fight for their rights and to achieve their goals.

Although Rutilio Grande did not directly get involved with FECCAS, he maintained that "while we cannot get married to political groups of any sort . . . we cannot remain indifferent to the politics of the common good of the vast majority of the peo-

Jesuit Father Rutilio Grande.
(Courtesy Maryknoll Archives)

ple." He understood that "as a result of the dynamism of conversion and growth in faith . . . Christians would normally become agents of change, as the church itself wants . . . working for unionization and defense of labor rights."

By 1975, Jesuits across the world had defined their mission as one that recognized an intimate link between the proclamation of faith and the promotion of justice. This confirmed the direction that Rutilio had taken in Aguilares.

Because of his commitment to the poor and to the peasants in Aguilares, Rutilio Grande repeatedly came under attack from right-wing groups. Even Colonel Molina, the president of El Salvador, who proposed a very moderate land reform, was attacked by the oligarchy, and eventually his plan was defeated.

As the conflict in Aguilares between peasants and landowners reached a point of crisis, the landowners began to publish advertisements in the newspapers denouncing FECCAS and the Jesuits. A right-wing death squad appeared, circulating leaflets that said: "Be a patriot, kill a priest!"

# The Death of Rutilio Grande

In February 1977, just one month before his assassination, Father Rutilio Grande preached a homily in the neighboring town of Apopa. One month before, Mario Bernal, the Colombian pastor of Apopa, had been kidnapped by security forces and deported to Guatemala. Grande's homily was characteristic of his style of relating events in El Salvador to biblical themes:

> It's practically illegal to be a true Christian in El Salvador. Because the world around us is radically based on an established disorder, before which the mere proclamation of the Gospel is subversive . . . I'm very afraid that soon the Bible and the Gospel won't be able to cross our borders. We'll just get the bindings because all the pages are subversive . . .
>
> I'm afraid that if Jesus of Nazareth came back, coming down from Galilee to Judea, that is, from Chalatenango to San Salvador, I daresay he would not get as far as Apopa, with his preaching and his actions. They would stop him in Guazapa and jail him there . . . They would accuse him of being a rabble-rouser, a foreign Jew, one confusing the people with strange and exotic ideas . . . They would undoubtedly crucify him again.
>
> In Christianity today you have to be ready to give up your life to serve a just order . . . to save others, for the values of the Gospel![81]

Events in El Salvador were taking a dramatic turn, as they were for the church. Luis Chávez y González, the archbishop of San Salvador, was about to retire after thirty-eight years, and tensions were running high as to who would be his successor. Chávez had left behind a clergy committed to the poor, and they backed the peasants' right to organize and to exert political pressure on the landowners and the government.

The clergy favored Arturo Rivera y Damas, who had been the auxiliary bishop since 1960, to succeed Chávez as archbishop. Chávez also favored Rivera y Damas. But Rome had other plans. They chose Romero as the new archbishop, siding with the wealthy landowners, government leaders, and military officers—more than forty in all—with whom the apostolic nuncio had consulted:

> We knew that Rome had been in consultation with various groups since late 1976 in the search for a new archbishop, knowing that Chávez had reached the age of retirement. The nuncio proposed Romero as a candidate and consulted with the government, the military, the business sector, and the ladies of society. They asked the rich, and the rich gave their complete backing to Romero's appointment. They felt he was "one of theirs."[82]

Prior to becoming archbishop, Romero had already begun to change. But faced with such opposition from within the church, he knew he needed help. On February 20, 1977, the day he was installed in a simple ceremony as archbishop, Romero sought to calm fears about his appointment by opening the door to dialogue with the priests of the archdiocese: "I wish to tell you of the spirit of cooperation that I offer you, and that I need from you, so that together we can share the honor that Christ gives us of helping him build his church, each one in his own vocation."[83]

Bishop Arturo Rivera y Damas, whom the clergy favored to become the archbishop of San Salvador. (Courtesy Maryknoll Archives)

That same day, after a fraudulent election, General Humberto Romero (no relation to Archbishop Romero) became president of El Salvador. One week later, on February 28, dozens of people protesting the outcome of the elections were assassinated by the military in the public square in front of El Rosario Church, just one block from the metropolitan cathedral in San Salvador.

The violence continued to spread over the next few weeks. Late in the afternoon of Saturday, March 12, Rutilio Grande was driving through the cane fields on his way to celebrate Mass in El Paisnal, a village near Aguilares. Accompanying him were Manuel Solorzano, an old peasant, and Nelson Rutilio Lemus, a teenager, and some children whom Grande was giving a lift to in his Safari jeep. Ambushers opened fire, instantly killing Grande, Solorzano, and Lemus, while the children escaped.

Later that night, as the bodies were laid out in the parish house,

Romero came to Aguilares to see with his own eyes what had happened. Ernestina Rivera, one of the women from the parish of Aguilares, offered this testimony of what transpired that night:

> I took off Father Grande's socks, all soaked with blood, and helped to undress him. He was dead. When I heard the news, I felt as if I was being picked up in the air and thrown down on the ground. I was so shaken that I don't even know how I got to the parish house. And now I ask myself how I lived through the events of the day. I loved him. That's why, to this day, I have saved a little piece of cloth soaked with his blood.
>
> The priests gave me permission to stay there the two nights that we held our wake for him in the parish house in Aguilares. All of us were gathered together remembering the wonderful communities that we had created with him.
>
> It was midnight when Monseñor Romero arrived to see his body. He approached the little table where we had him, wrapped in a white sheet, and there he paused, looking at him in a way that made me see that he loved him too. I didn't know Monseñor then. That night we heard his voice for the first time, preaching. When we heard him, it was a great surprise.
>
> "Ay! Even his voice is just like Father Grande's." That's what we all said. Because it seemed to us that right there, the words of Father Rutilio had been passed to Monseñor. Right there. Truly.
>
> "Is it possible that God has worked this miracle so that we will not be left as orphans?" my comadre whispered to me.[84]

The Cathedral of San Salvador.
(Courtesy Maryknoll Archives)

On March 14, two days after Rutilio Grande's assassination, Romero joined more than one hundred priests in the funeral Mass before an overflowing crowd in San Salvador. Romero chose as a reading the Gospel of John: "No greater love is there than to give one's life out of love for one's friends" (John 15:13).

If this were an ordinary funeral, he said, he would speak of his friendship with Rutilio Grande: "At peak moments of my life he was very close to me, and those gestures are never forgotten." But

this was no ordinary funeral, it was a moment "to gather from this death a message for all of us who remain on pilgrimage."[85]

Romero read words from Paul VI's apostolic exhortation *Evangelii Nuntiandi* and proclaimed to the crowd: "The Church cannot be absent from the struggle for liberation," but its original contribution is to offer three things: "the inspiration of faith, the social doctrine . . . and, above all, a motivation of love."

The inspiration of faith offers a spiritual horizon to the struggle for liberation. The social doctrine "looks to God, and from God looks to our neighbor as a brother or sister," and "organizes life according to the heart of God." The motivation of love motivates us to give our lives for others. In sum, Rutilio Grande embodied all three of these, and "died loving others," pardoning his enemies.

Mass for Father Rutilio Grande in the Cathedral of San Salvador, March 1977. (Courtesy Equipo Maíz)

*"Who knows if the murderers that have now fallen into excommunication are listening to a radio in their hideout, listening, in their conscience to this word. We want to tell you, murderous brothers, that we love you and that we ask of God repentance for your hearts, because the church is not able to hate."*

# Crossing the Threshold

ollowing the assassination of Rutilio Grande, Romero
agonized about how to respond. Then he made a
momentous decision. He wrote to the out-going president of El Salvador, Colonel Molina, and informed him that he
was "not willing to participate in any official act of the government as long as the latter did not put all its effort into making
justice manifest in regard to this unprecedented sacrilege,
which had horrified the whole church and stirred up in the
country a new wave of repudiation of violence."[86]

Romero also accepted a proposal to cancel all masses in the
archdiocese the following Sunday, March 20, and to celebrate a
single Mass in the metropolitan cathedral of San Salvador as a
show of solidarity and protest for the killing of Rutilio Grande
and his two companions.

But the decision to hold a single Mass in the cathedral—and to
cancel all other masses in the archdiocese—was a struggle for
Romero, and reflected his concerns about how the Salvadoran government and the Vatican would interpret it. He encountered sharp
opposition from the other bishops and from the nuncio, who scold-
ed Romero, and called him irresponsible and imprudent.

Romero tried to explain to the nuncio that "the single
Eucharist of the archdiocese gathered around its pastor was a
unique opportunity to bring all the faithful into that unity."[87]
But the nuncio would have nothing to do with it, and Romero
refused to back down.

Still, Romero had his doubts. He decided to meet again with
the priests from the archdiocese, and with a few women religious. He asked them to discuss whether he should go forward
with the "single Mass," and to vote on the decision. César Jerez,
the Jesuit provincial for Central America at that time, was present, and reported on the meeting:

"And do you really think that it would do any good?"
Monseñor Romero was full of doubts. He wanted to be

*"The violence we preach is not
the violence of the sword, the
violence of hatred. It is the
violence of love, of brotherhood,
the violence that wills to beat
weapons into sickles for work."*
—November 27, 1977

46

convinced, to hear all of the arguments, to arrive at a truly collective decision . . .

"The government is going to interpret this Mass as a provocation!"

"It will be a provocation. An open-air Mass with a crowd of people in the streets during this state of siege . . . We can't guarantee that there won't be shots fired and that this won't end up in a slaughter!"

"But the people in the communities are already in favor of holding a single Mass!"

Monseñor Romero was full of reservations. He finally came out with what appeared to be his biggest concern.

"And in this situation, wouldn't we be giving greater glory to God by having many Masses in different places than a single Mass in a single place?"

The pros and cons were argued out again. After a while, I asked to speak.

"You know, I think that all of us here think that a Mass is an act of infinite value. So does it make any sense to be worried about saying a bunch of Masses? Are we

Romero with Jesuits of the Central American University: theologian Jon Sobrino on the left, Segundo Montes (later assassinated with other members of his community) on the right. (Courtesy Jon Sobrino, S.J.)

47

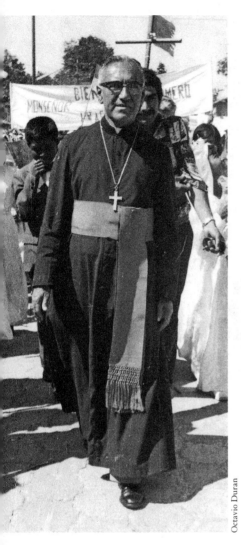

Octavio Duran

trying to add up the infinites? One is enough. I think that Monseñor Romero is absolutely right that we should be concerned about the glory of God, but if I remember right, the bishop and martyr Saint Irenaeus once said, *'Gloria Dei vivens homo'*—'The glory of God is the living person.'"

I think that argument finally convinced him. In the end, with the approval of the great majority of those gathered, it was decided that on Sunday, March 20, there would be only one Mass, a single Mass, in the whole Archdiocese of San Salvador.[88]

When the vote was finally taken, seventy-one voted in favor, one against, and one abstained. The decision was made, and the archdiocese went forward with its plan for the single Mass—what became known as *"la misa unica."*

The following Sunday, a hundred thousand people filled the plaza in front of the metropolitan cathedral in San Salvador, the largest demonstration of Salvadoran church unity in recent memory.[89] In his homily, Romero spoke of the meaning of the Mass, and when he mentioned the name "Padre Grande," the crowd erupted in applause.

This response of approval would be the beginning of a new relationship between pastor and people, and would occur many times during the next three years every time Romero preached the Sunday Mass in the cathedral. It was a sign that the Word of God had truly been received by the people, it had "become flesh," and illumined their journey through "the desert," like a pillar of fire. Three more times during Romero's homily, the crowd erupted in applause.

Inocencio Alas, one of the Salvadoran priests who was present that day, recounts how Romero's words sealed his conversion. He had "crossed the threshold":

The plaza was full to overflowing. More than 100,000 people were there, and who knows how many more were listening on their radios. The priests dispersed into the crowd, and hundreds of people were saying their confessions on the streets. Many people who had distanced themselves from the Church for years, returned to their faith that day. Rutilio's assassination and the message given by that single Mass were alarms sounding, waking people up. Almost all of the priests of the archdiocese concelebrated that day—about 150 of us—as well as priests from other dioceses who overcame all obstacles to be there.

As the Mass began, I noticed that Monseñor Romero was sweating, pale, and nervous. And when he began the homily, it seemed slow to me, without his usual eloquence, as if he was reluctant to go through the door of history that God was opening for him. But after about five minutes, I felt the Holy Spirit descend upon him.

"... I want to give a public thanks today, here in front of the archdiocese, for the unified support that is being expressed for the Gospel and for these our beloved priests. Many of them are in danger, and like Father Grande, they are risking even the maximum sacrifice ..."

Hearing the name of Rutilio, thousands exploded into applause.

"This applause confirms the profound joy that my heart feels upon taking possession of the archdiocese and feeling that my own weaknesses and my own inabilities can find their complement, their strength, and their courage in a united clergy. Whoever touches one of my priests, is touching me. And they will have to deal with me!"

Thousands of people were applauding him, and something rose within him. It was then that he crossed the threshold. He went through the door. Because, you know, there is baptism by water, and there is baptism by blood. But there is also baptism by the people.[90]

*"I ask the faithful people who listen to me with love and devotion to pardon me for saying this, but it gives me more pleasure that my enemies listen to me. I know that the reason they listen to me is that I bear them a message of love. I don't hate them. I don't want revenge. I wish them no harm. I beg them to be converted, to come to be happy with the happiness that you faithful ones have."*
—January 15, 1978

# Coming Home Again

Much is made of the "conversion" of Oscar Romero to the poor upon the death of his friend, Father Rutilio Grande, who was assassinated on March 12, 1977. The word "conversion" is used to mean "a turning point" in Romero's life.

Jon Sobrino makes this point: "I think that, as Archbishop Romero stood gazing at the mortal remains of Rutilio Grande, the scales fell from his eyes."[91] Ignacio Martin-Baro, one of the six Jesuit martyrs, makes a similar point: "For Romero, the assassination of Father Grande . . . was the crucial moment in his conversion: the road to Aguilares was to be his road to Damascus."[92]

Bishop Arturo Rivera y Damas, who succeeded Romero as Archbishop of San Salvador, also believes the death of Rutilio Grande was the key moment in Romero's transformation:

> One martyr gave life to another martyr. Before the cadaver of Father Rutilio Grande, Monseñor Romero, in his twentieth day as archbishop, felt that call of Christ to overcome his natural human timidity and to be filled with the fortitude of the apostle. From that moment, Monseñor Romero left behind the pagan lands of Tyre and Sidon and marched with freedom toward Jerusalem.[93]

What actually transpired in that moment? Sobrino writes the following:

> After Mass, Archbishop Romero asked us priests and sisters to remain in the church . . . He was visibly agitated. He seemed to be laboring under the responsibility of having to do something and not knowing exactly what to do . . . He must have been afraid . . . The hour had come in which he would have to face up to the powerful—the oligarchy and the government . . .
>
> I also felt, or seemed to surmise, that something very profound was transpiring deep within Archbishop

*"To each one of us Christ is saying: If you want your life and mission to be fruitful like mine, do like me. Be converted into a seed that lets itself be buried. Let yourself be killed. Do not be afraid. Those who shun suffering will remain alone. No one is more alone than the selfish. But if you give your life out of love for others, as I give mine for all, you will reap a great harvest. You will have the deepest satisfactions. Do not fear death or threats. The Lord goes with you."*

*—April 1, 1979*

Romero . . . I think he was forming the high resolve to react in whatever way God might ask: he was making an authentic option for the poor, who had been represented, a scant hour before, by hundreds of campesinos gathered about three corpses, helpless in the face of the repression they had already suffered and knowing full well that there was more to come . . .

Romero on a picnic with seminarians. (Octavio Duran)

I believe that those campesinos had made an option for [Romero]—that they were asking him to defend them. And his response was to make an option for the campesinos—to be converted and transformed into their defender, to become the voice of the voiceless. I believe that Archbishop Romero's definitive conversion began that night.[94]

Kevin Burke, SJ, takes this intuition one step further, and links the meaning of "conversion" to what it means to have "a resurrection experience" and "to live as risen beings."[95]

Romero himself may or may not have thought to call the

Romero celebrates Mass behind an altar bearing the images of martyred Salvadoran priests. (Octavio Duran)

experience in Aguilares "a resurrection experience." My argument is not based on a retrieval of Romero's own interpretation of that night. Rather, this is my interpretation based on the logic of resurrection encounters as depicted in the gospels and elaborated by Paul.

There are four images connected to that night in Aguilares and its aftermath to which I call attention: Romero standing in the presence of three martyrs; his need to say something, to speak out on behalf of his people; his desire to work at reconciliation; and the fact that all this occurs in a Eucharistic experience.[96]

Romero's conversion might also be likened to a call to share the Good News of God's grace with his people. Like Paul, who shared the Good News of Jesus Christ with the Gentiles, Romero announced the Good News to the poor in a way that was new and profoundly life-giving.

There was surprise, nevertheless, at what occurred that night, and what it signified in Romero's life once he had become archbishop. Sobrino continues:

Whether one actually calls it a conversion or not, the radical change that took place in Archbishop Romero on the occasion of Rutilio's murder was one of the most impressive things anyone around him, including myself, had ever seen. He was fifty-nine years old at the time, an age at which people's psychological and mental structure, their understanding of the faith, their spirituality, and their Christian commitment have typically hardened . . .

If Archbishop Romero set out on new paths, at his age, in his place at the pinnacle of the institution, and against such odds, then his conversion must have been very real. It must have reached the deepest corners of his being, shaping him for good and all, and leading him to the sacrifice of his life.[97]

Monseñor Ricardo Urioste, one of Romero's closest friends, compares Romero's transformation to that of the blind man in the Gospel of Mark (8:22–26) who, when Jesus laid his hands on his eyes, saw everything clearly. Father Ignacio Ellacuría also described Romero's transformation as something objective, a new sight and a new truth that took possession of him.[98]

Months later, César Jerez, the Jesuit provincial, accompanied Romero to Rome and recalled this conversation:

"Monseñor, you've changed. Everything about you has changed. What's happened?"

"You know, Father Jerez, I ask myself that same question when I'm in prayer." He stopped walking and was silent . . . "It's just that we all have our roots, you know . . . I was born into a poor family. I've suffered hunger . . . When I went to seminary [in Rome] . . . I started to forget about where I came from. I started creating another world. When I went back to El Salvador, they made me the bishop's secretary in San Miguel . . ."

We were walking slowly. It seemed like he wanted to keep talking. "Then they sent me to Santiago de María, and I ran into extreme poverty again. Those children were dying just because of the water they were drinking, those campesinos killing themselves in the harvests . . . And what happened to Father Grande . . . You know how much I admired him. When I saw Rutilio dead, I thought, 'If they killed him for what he was doing, it's my job to go down that same road . . .' So yes, I changed. But I also came back home again."

We kept walking in silence. The light from the new moon accented the Roman sky.[99]

*"I am glad, brothers and sisters, that our church is persecuted precisely for its preferential option for the poor and for trying to become incarnate on behalf of he poor. And I want to say to all the people, to rulers, to the rich and powerful: If you do not become poor, if you do not concern yourselves for the poverty of our people, as though they were your own family, you will not be able to save society."*
—July 15, 1979

# The Paschal Hour

Pope Paul VI. (Fotografia Pontifica)

Romero decided to make a visit to Rome on March 26, 1977, to consult with the pope. He was accompanied by Monseñor Ricardo Urioste, who became a close confidant. Upon his arrival, he went to visit the tomb of St. Peter.

All of the commotion in El Salvador over Rutilio Grande's death, and the changes in [Romero] that were reflected in his first steps as archbishop, had sounded an alarm in the offices of the Vatican. I made the trip with him. We arrived in Rome at midday. Soon after we had gotten settled in our rooms, there was a knock on my door.

"Do you want to go for a little walk?"

He wanted to go to St. Peter's Basilica, so I went with him. When we arrived, he went straight to one of the altars. We knelt, and soon I could see that Monseñor Romero had entered into a deep state of prayer. It was as if he was laying all of the worries of his recent work as archbishop before the tomb of Peter, the first Pope.

After kneeling for ten minutes, I had to stand up, but he stayed there in the same position, without moving, in complete concentration. He remained like that for another quarter of an hour. Afterwards we left and began to talk about what lay ahead of us.[100]

The high point of his visit was his brief encounter with Pope Paul VI. Romero went to his general audience, and the pope singled him out and introduced him to the group. Then he pulled him aside and took him to another room for a private talk: "Courage! You're the one in charge," he told Romero.[101]

Upon his return to San Salvador, Romero continued working on a pastoral letter for Easter. He called it "The Easter Church." The Archdiocese of San Salvador was living a "paschal hour" coinciding with the liturgical season and the events surrounding his installation as archbishop. The archdiocese was responding to what the Latin American bishops had urged at Medellín: "We are on the threshold of a new epoch in the history of our continent. It appears to be a time full of zeal for full emancipation, of liberation from every form of servitude, of personal maturity, and of collective integration."[102]

Romero was beginning to make a home for himself in the archdiocese, and one of the first things he did was to take up residence on the grounds of the Divine Providence Hospital, a residential care facility for terminal cancer patients. It was here, three years later, that Archbishop Romero would be assassinated, celebrating Mass in the chapel on the hospital grounds.

Archbishop Romero lived in this small house on the grounds of a cancer hospital from August 1977 until his death. (James Brockman, S.J.)

> He decided to come live with us at the "Hospitalito"— that's what everyone calls it. It's the Divine Providence Hospital; patients with terminal cancer are cared for here.
>
> We sisters had a long-standing friendship with Monseñor Romero; we had known him since the time when he was a priest in San Miguel. Then, when he was bishop in Santiago de María, he started the custom of coming to say Mass for us on the first of each month. And when he had meetings at the Bishops' Conference, he would come and have dinner with us, and sometimes he'd stay and sleep here in the sacristy. I don't know why, but he was fond of this place. Soon after he was named archbishop, he came to ask us if he could live here, and our community was very proud to be asked.[103]

Romero also established a Legal Aid Office, which played an important role in documenting the human rights abuses and providing testimony for his Sunday homilies.

> Whenever I went to Monseñor Romero's office to work on the legal case concerning the assassination of Father Rutilio Grande, he would always start up another conversation when we were done.
>
> "Tell me about *Servicio Juridico*," he said with great interest.
>
> Two years earlier, a group of lawyers including myself had gotten involved in this effort. We provided legal services on land rights issues, common causes, family struggles,

Romero recording a broadcast for the archdiocesan radio station.
(Octavio Duran)

*"If some day they take the radio station away from us, if they close down our newspaper, if they don't let us speak, if they kill all the priests and the bishop too, and you are left, a people without priests, each one of you must be God's microphone, each one of you must be a messenger, a prophet."* —July 8, 1979

notary services, and all of those kinds of things that so many poor people usually couldn't afford. Monseñor fell in love with the project and dreamed about making it part of the archdiocese. Finally, he was able to do that. Then the name changed to Socorro Juridico—Legal Aid. In the same way, he kept bringing new projects, efforts and people under the protective umbrella of the archdiocese.[104]

In addition to the Legal Aid Office, Romero revived the archdiocesan radio station, YSAX. Since he had been a parish priest in San Miguel, he had developed radio programs to more effectively communicate with his parishioners. Letters from remote villages became another channel of communication between Romero and the people.

Nobody knew how to read or write in those remote villages, and still the letters poured in. From the very beginning, letters came to the archdiocese like never before. All of them were addressed to Monseñor Romero. That had never happened before. The other novelty was that many of the letters came from campesino communities where the letters were written collectively. Someone who knew how to write would write in the name of the whole group . . . But they almost never arrived through the postal system . . . The parish priests would bring the letters in by hand.

Monseñor's radio homilies, his frequent visits to the communities and these letters provided a framework for extensive communication between the bishop and the people. And it wasn't just the people of the Archdiocese of San Salvador, the ones in his own flock, it was people all over the country . . .

"Leave the letters out for me. I want to read them . . ." He liked to be able to read them personally, but he couldn't always do that.[105]

On May 11, just two months after the assassination of Rutilio Grande, a second priest, Alfonso Navarro, was killed in retaliation for the kidnapping and murder of the Salvadoran foreign minister. Four men entered the rectory of Resurrection parish in San Salvador and shot Navarro and a young boy. Navarro died, according to a witness, pardoning his assassins.[106]

Two hundred priests came to concelebrate his funeral Mass. The radio station YSAX carried Romero's homily, which began:

*They tell how a caravan, guided by a desert Bedouin, was desperate with thirst and sought water in the mirages of the desert. The guide kept saying, "No, not that way, this way." This happened several times, until one of the caravan, his patience exhausted, took out a pistol and shot the guide, who, dying, stretched out his hand to say, "Not that way—this way." And so he died, pointing the way. The legend becomes a reality: a priest [Navarro], pierced with bullets, who dies pardoning, who dies praying, gives his message to all of us who at this hour unite for his burial.*[107]

Navarro's message, Romero continued, was "a protest, a rejection of violence: 'They kill me because I point the way to follow.' And we, the church, repeat once more that violence resolves nothing, violence is not Christian, not human." Romero concluded the homily with an appeal to unity:

*This is not the hour, brothers and sisters, to be divided into two churches. It is the hour to feel ourselves one church that strives for Christ's resurrection, that brings redemption not only beyond death but here on earth; to strive for a world more just, more human; to strive for a social sensitivity that makes itself felt in every setting; to struggle against violence, against criminality.*[108]

Father Alfonso Navarro, assassinated on May 11, 1977. (Courtesy Maryknoll Archives)

# Aguilares

Octavio Duran

On May 19, 1977, government troops began to evict at gunpoint peasant families that had occupied land on the Hacienda San Francisco in El Paisnal. About five hundred campesinos who had been renting little plots of previously uncultivated land were demanding a lower rent so they could afford to plant their corn. Two thousand soldiers with armored cars surrounded the town of Aguilares, ransacking houses, raping women, and arresting men and women. At least fifty people were disappeared.[109]

The National Guard desecrated the church in Aguilares and used it as a barracks. Soldiers shot open the tabernacle and strewed the hosts on the floor. The three Jesuits who worked in Aguilares were detained and later deported. Romero tried to go to Aguilares but was prevented from doing so. Tensions between the government and the church reached a new low. Romero wrote:

*We consider these deeds a clear proof that the government of the republic is bent on depriving the Catholic people of El Salvador of those priests who are committed to the service of the people. Persecution of the church is justified in the name of the struggle against atheistic communism. Some affirm that no such persecution exists. But in light of the facts and of the threats that hang over certain priests, to us and to the immense majority of the Catholic people the persecution is very clear.*[110]

Aguilares remained militarized for a month. On June 19, the army left, and Archbishop Romero went to Aguilares to celebrate Mass, accompanied by the basic Christian communities of San Salvador. During the military occupation, two hundred people were assassinated, tortured, and disappeared. Most of the people who filled the church for Mass that day were not from Aguilares.

I recall the great love Archbishop Romero showed for those campesinos of Aguilares, those suffering, terrified people, who had experienced such awful things over the previous month. How could they be helped to maintain their hope? How could they be given back at least their dignity in suffering? How could they be told that they were the most important thing to God and the church? Archbishop Romero put it this way: "You are the image of the divine victim 'pierced for our offenses,' of whom the first reading speaks to us this morning. You are Christ today, suffering in history."[111]

Romero went on to identify himself and the church with those who had suffered so much during the military occupation, especially those who had lost loved ones, those who were being tortured, those who had to flee. When he finished, five thousand people applauded his words. Then he introduced the new pastoral team to those present.

After the Mass, the people accompanied Romero and the Blessed Sacrament in a procession around the town square. As they passed the town hall, National Guardsmen confronted them, pointing their weapons at the crowd. Jon Sobrino recalled that tense moment vividly:

*La Opinion* was published solely to attack Archbishop Romero. This headline accuses him of promoting terrorism in his sermons. (Courtesy Maryknoll Archives)

> We left the church singing. It was a terribly hot day, and Monseñor Romero was soaked in sweat under his red rain cape. He held the monstrance high. Before him, there were hundreds of people. We circled the main square singing and praying. The municipal offices across from the church were full of guardsmen watching us. When we neared, several of them went to the middle of the road and pointed their rifles at us. Then more of them came. They spread their legs defiantly and with their large boots formed a wall that we could not go through.
>
> Those at the front stopped and gradually so did those further back. The procession came to a halt. There we were, face to face with the rifles. When no one was moving anymore, we turned to look at Monseñor Romero, who was at the very back. He lifted the monstrance a little higher and said in a loud voice so that all could hear: "Adelante"—"Let us go forward."
>
> Then, little by little, we moved toward the soldiers, and little by little, they began to back up. We moved forward. They moved backward. Eventually they backed up

Romero visiting a village in Chalatenango. (Octavio Duran)

toward their barracks. Finally, they lowered their rifles and let us pass.

From that day on, when any important event occurred in El Salvador, whether you were with him or against him, you always had to look to Monseñor Romero.[112]

On June 21, the White Warrior Union, a paramilitary death squad, issued a warning to all Jesuits to leave the country within thirty days or become "military targets." The threat was taken seriously since one Jesuit had been assassinated and three others deported, in addition to six bombs exploding on the Jesuit campus during the previous year.

Meanwhile, preparations were going on for the installation of the new president of El Salvador, General Carlos Humberto Romero, which would take place on July 1. Archbishop Romero kept his promise not to attend any official government functions, since the assassination of Rutilio Grande had never been investigated. The apostolic nuncio, however, and two bishops did attend the inauguration.

Nearly six months had passed since Romero had become archbishop. He had confronted serious problems, including the assassination of two priests and the military occupation of Aguilares. Yet he had come home again, as he had confided to César Jerez; he was on his way down the same road that Rutilio Grande had walked. And he continued to preach the Gospel with courage and conviction:

> The true protagonists of history are those most united with God, because with God's viewpoint they can best attend to the signs of the times, the ways of Providence, the building of history. Oh, if we only had persons of prayer among those who oversee the fate of the nation and the fate of the economy! If, instead of relying on human devices, people would rely on God and on his devices, we would have a world like the one the church dreams of, a world without injustices, a world with respect for rights, a world with generous participation by all, a world without repression, a world without torture.[113]

# The Body of Christ in History

On August 6, 1977, the feast of the Transfiguration and El Salvador's patron feast, Archbishop Romero published his second pastoral letter, "The Church, Body of Christ in History." He had already published one pastoral letter, "The Easter Church," five months earlier, and he would publish two more before his assassination in 1980. He asked Jon Sobrino to write a first draft, then he rewrote it, retaining the basic argument and outline of the letter.[114]

Romero begins his letter boldly and confidently asserting the church's mission in the world:

> *Many things in the church have changed in recent years . . . But the fundamental change, the change that explains all the others, is the new relationship between the church and the world. The church looks upon the world with new eyes. It will raise questions about what is sinful in the world, and it will also allow itself to be questioned by the world as to what is sinful in the church.*[115]

The relation between the church and the world was a fundamental theme of all four pastoral letters, but with a caveat: Romero was "absolutely serious about the [concrete] historical reality" of his time. That was the challenge that he faced, and the legacy that he left us.

We may ask ourselves, what is the significance of his letters and talks 30 years later? Undoubtedly, someone will say that things have changed, which is true. But . . . what Romero said about the idols and the victims, and the need for justice and truth, is absolutely essential today.[116]

According to Sobrino, in all of his letters Romero was guided by the Gospel: "In the Gospel he discovered the fundamental criteria for a church that continues the works of Jesus, announcing its faith in the God of Jesus and incarnating itself in the concrete world of the poor. This was fundamental to Romero's thinking, such that he was convinced that the Word

Octavio Duran

of God has a specific impact. 'The Word of God is not enchained,' he would say."[117]

Romero also made abundant use of the teaching of the church, especially the Second Vatican Council, the social encyclicals of Paul VI, and the teachings of Medellín and Puebla.

*"A preaching that does not point out sin is not the preaching of the gospel. A preaching that makes sinners feel good so that they become entrenched in their sinful state betrays the gospel's call . . . A preaching that awakens, a preaching that enlightens—as when a light turned on awakens and of course annoys a sleeper—that is the preaching of Christ, calling Wake up! Be converted!"* —January 22, 1978

Romero used these teachings, not routinely, but with audacity, creativity and commitment: With audacity, for example he cited passages about themes—such as the right to grassroots organizing, violence, dialogue with Marxist groups, the social mortgage on private property—that generated great conflict in our country . . . With creativity . . . for example he developed the pastoral ministry of accompaniment, which was truly new . . . With commitment . . . [h]e said: "It's very easy to speak of the church's Social Teaching, but difficult to put it into practice, knowing that attacks and persecution will follow."[118]

In a country profoundly divided by wealth and poverty, it was no surprise to Romero that his words cut like a two-edged sword. His goal, however, was not to divide but to unify and to heal.

*The events of recent months remind us that Christian unity comes not only from a verbal confession of the same faith, but also from putting that faith into practice. It arises out of a common effort, a shared mission. It comes from fidelity to the Word and to the demands of Jesus Christ, and it is cemented in common suffering. Unity in the church is not achieved by ignoring the reality of the world in which we live . . . We cannot, as the price of unity, abandon our mission. Let us remember that what divides us is not the church's actions but the world's sin—and the sin of our society.*[119]

What did Romero hope to accomplish in this second pastoral letter?

*What I am going to say here is not at all new. But I believe it is desirable to repeat it because it has not been sufficiently assimilated and because in our country many voices, on the radio and in the newspapers, presume to judge what the church is, distorting its true nature and mission.*[120]

Romero understood that without truth, there could be no

Octavio Duran

justice. His weekly homilies and annual pastoral letters were attempts to present the truth of the Gospel and the church's social teaching amid the political turmoil of the nation. His words had the power of truth in a country where the media was controlled by the government and given to falsifying reality in favor of the wealthy and powerful.

The church must be a concrete embodiment of what the Synod of Bishops proclaimed in 1971 when they wed social justice to the Gospel.

Action on behalf of justice and participation in the transformation of the world fully appear to us as a constitutive dimension of the preaching of the Gospel . . . and the church's mission for the redemption of the human race and its liberation from every oppressive situation.[121]

No longer timid about citing Medellín, Romero reaffirms those teachings in his second pastoral letter in order to defend the mission of the church in El Salvador in an increasingly hostile and conflictive environment.

*When Medellín attempts to sum up in one phrase, what for our continent is the fundamental sin of the age, it has no hesitation in asserting that it is "that misery, which as a collective fact, expresses itself as injustice which cries to heaven."*[122]

In such a decisive moment in history, the desperate poverty of the poor and their longings for liberation challenged the church to respond in solidarity:

*The Church is in the world . . . to bring into being the liberating love of God manifested in Christ. It therefore understands Christ's preference for the poor, because the poor are, as Medellín explains, those who "place before the Latin American Church a challenge and a mission that it cannot sidestep and to which it must respond with a speed and boldness adequate to the urgency of the times."*[123]

In all of his pastoral letters and in his homilies, Romero did what the Magisterium had taught, consulting with his people "to analyze with objectivity the situation proper to their country, to shed on it the light of the Gospel's unalterable words, and to draw principles of reflection, norms of judgment and directives for action from the social teaching of the Church."[124]

Romero knew, however, that by shedding the light of the Gospel on the social reality of his country, he was inviting persecution, for there were some who "pretended not to hear the voice of Vatican II and of Medellín," those who "were scandalized at the Church's new face."[125]

*"I repeat what I told you once before when we feared we might be left without a radio station: God's best microphone is Christ, and Christ's best microphone is the church, and the church is all of you."*

—January 27, 1980

# The Sky Has Turned Red

Romero is interviewed by a journalist.
(Octavio Duran)

Archbishop Romero did not have to wait long before there was a response to his August 6 pastoral letter. On August 9, General Romero's private secretary appeared with an invitation to Archbishop Romero to meet with the president the following afternoon. Despite the archbishop's promise not to appear in public events with the government until the assassination of Rutilio Grande was investigated, he was always open to dialogue in private with government officials.

Before he became president, General Romero had been Minister of Defense and Public Security under President Molina and, as such, was responsible for the violence and repression carried out against the people. Now he spoke of "slight differences" between the government and the church and called for dialogue.[126]

Archbishop Romero handed the president a memorandum he had drafted, calling for cooperation between the church and the government. He also gave copies of the Medellín documents to high government and military leaders. In subsequent meetings, General Romero lamented that the traditional alliance between the church, capitalists, and the military had broken down, and the church had gone its own way.[127]

The government, however, never had any real interest in cooperating, and the attacks and violence continued throughout the country. On November 3, soldiers skirmished with a group on the outskirts of Osicala, in the eastern department of Morazán. In reprisal, they arrested Father Miguel Ventura, the pastor of the church, and subjected him to torture, tying his arms behind him and hanging him from a tree limb. The sacristan of the parish was also tortured.[128]

Archbishop Romero lamented the continuing persecution of the church the following Sunday and formally pronounced the excommunication of those who had laid violent hands on the priest. Ventura's bishop, Eduardo Alvarez, a military chaplain, told his fellow bishops that Ventura had acted in the area of politics and therefore suffered the consequences.[129] When asked about the incident, Alvarez replied: "But you see, Father Miguel was tortured as a man, not as a priest."[130]

Fabio Argueta, one of the catechists who went to see Father Ventura after he had been released, was himself detained and subjected to beatings and electric shock over a period of several weeks. When he was released, he met with Romero.

*"The hour of trial will pass and the ideal so many Christians died for will survive resplendent. It is a black night that we are living, but Christianity discerns that beyond the night the dawn already glows. The hope that does not fail is carried in the heart, Christ goes with us!"*
*—September 23, 1979*

"The crime they're accusing me of," I told Monseñor, "is that of preaching the Gospel." Then I told him that ever since I'd participated in the courses at the El Castaño Center a few years earlier, I'd come to believe what we'd been taught there: that the injustices we suffer as poor people were an offense to God, a sin that had to be done away with.

"From that idea alone, we received strength, Monseñor. And you know the saying, 'If the horse already flies, it doesn't need spurs.' What's happening now is that they're trying to rein us in by torturing us."

"People who torture their fellow human beings are agents of the devil." Monseñor was both sad and serious as he told this to me. And from there, he started to tell me the history of the church, chapter by chapter. He spoke to me about this path called the "option for the poor" and how choosing this path had brought us so much persecution. I remember very well a sentence he kept repeating.

"Putting ourselves on the side of the poor is going to mean a lot of bloodshed for us. All this blood is a sign of the times . . ."

"How long will this last, Monseñor . . . ?

"We don't know. We have to look up to the heavens and know how to read the signs. Right now we have this: In El Salvador the sky has turned red. We don't know how long it will last."[131]

On November 24, the government passed a draconian Law for Defense of Public Order, giving them the right to detain suspects for "any presumption or indication" of participation in forbidden activity. Such a rationale allowed them a legal cover to torture and disappear anyone they chose.

Romero responded forcefully to this measure in his Sunday homily: "I am not an expert on law . . . From the theological, priestly viewpoint, however, in the light of God's word, I do have the right and the duty to cast light on this event in our land." He then proceeded to explain the teaching of Saint Thomas Aquinas on law: a real law must be just and must be for the society's common good, promulgated by a legitimate authority, and made public. He further quoted Saint Augustine: "A law that is not just should not call itself a law."[132]

One of the countless victims of violence is buried in the countryside. (Courtetsy Maryknoll Archives)

One sign of hope was the formation of a group of mothers of disappeared persons. Romero celebrated a Mass for them on December 1. Hundreds of people had been disappeared by this time in El Salvador, detained by the military or death squads, presumably tortured and likely killed.

Romero took up the defense of these disappeared and encouraged their mothers. He proposed the mother in the book of Maccabees, who encouraged her seven sons to die rather than to betray their faith, and Mary, who stood at the foot of the cross, as models of faith.[133]

> *Like Mary at the foot of the cross, every mother who suffers the outrage done to her child is an accusation. Mary, the sorrowing mother, before the power of Pontius Pilate, who has unjustly killed her son, is the cry of justice, of love, of peace, of what God wills, in the face of what God does not will, in the face of outrage, in the face of what should not be . . .*
>
> *This is the voice of justice, this is the voice of love, this is the cry that the church takes up from so many wives, mothers, homes, forsaken ones, in order to say: this should not be, return these sons and daughters as the law of God, the law of the Lord, demands. This is to cry out against sin. This is what the church is doing, crying out against the sin that enthrones itself in history, in the life of the nation.* [134]

# Following the Star

## Excerpts from Romero's Homilies

**First Sunday in Advent**

*When we preach the Lord's word,*
*we decry not only the injustices of the social order.*
*We decry every sin that is night, that is darkness:*
     *drunkenness, gluttony, lust, adultery, abortion,*
          *everything that is the reign of iniquity and sin.*
*Let them all disappear from our society . . .*

*We cannot segregate God's word*
*from the historical reality in which it is proclaimed.*
*It would not then be God's word.*
*It would be history,*
*it would be a pious book,*
     *a Bible that is just a book in our library.*
*It becomes God's word*
*because it vivifies,*
*enlightens, contrasts,*
*repudiates, praises*
     *what is going on today in this society . . .*

*We have never preached violence,*
*except the violence of love,*
*which left Christ nailed to a cross,*
     *the violence that we must each do to ourselves*
     *to overcome our selfishness*
     *and such cruel inequalities among us.*
*The violence we preach is not the violence of the sword,*
     *the violence of hatred.*
*It is the violence of love,*
     *of brotherhood,*
*the violence that wills to beat weapons*
*into sickles for work . . .*

**Second Sunday in Advent**

*A religion of Sunday Mass but of unjust weeks*
*does not please the Lord.*
*A religion of much praying but with hypocrisy in the heart*
*is not Christian.*
*A church that sets itself up only to be well off,*
*to have a lot of money and comfort,*
*but that forgets to protest injustices,*
*would not be the true church of our divine Redeemer . . .*

**Third Sunday in Advent**

*The church's task in each country*
*is to make of each country's individual history*
*a history of salvation . . .*

*What beautiful coffee groves,*
*what fine cane and cotton fields,*
*what farms, what lands God has given us!*
*Nature is so beautiful!*

*But we see it groan*
*under oppression,*
*under wickedness,*
*under injustice,*
*under abuse,*
*and the church feels its pain.*

Scott Wright

*Nature looks for a liberation*
*that will not be mere material well-being*
*but God's act of power.*

*God will free nature from sinful human hands,*
*and along with the redeemed it will sing a hymn of joy*
*to God the Liberator.*

**Fourth Sunday in Advent**

*Faith consists in accepting God*
*without asking him to account for things*
*according to our standard.*
*Faith consists in reacting before God as Mary did:*

*I don't understand it, Lord,*
*but let it be done in me according to your word . . .*

*Who knows if the one whose hands are bloodied*
*with Father Grande's murder,*
*or the one who shot Father Navarro,*
*if those who have killed, who have tortured,*
*who have done so much evil, are listening to me?*
*Listen, there in your criminal hideout,*
*perhaps already repentant,*
*you too are called to forgiveness . . .*

*When we struggle for human rights,*
*for freedom,*
*for dignity,*
*when we feel that it is a ministry of the church*
*to concern itself for those who are hungry,*
*for those who are deprived,*
*we are not departing from God's promise.*
*He comes to free us from sin,*
*and the church knows that sin's consequences*
*are all such injustices and abuses.*
*The church knows it is saving the world*
*when it undertakes to speak also of such things.*

### Christmas

*With Christ, God has injected himself into history. With the birth of Christ, God's reign is now inaugurated in human time.*

*On this night, as every year for twenty centuries, we recall that God's reign is now in this world and that Christ has inaugurated the fullness of time. His birth attests that God is now marching with us in history so that we do not go alone.*

*Humans long for peace, for justice, for a reign of divine law, for something holy, for what is far from earth's realities. We can have such a hope, not because we ourselves are able to construct the realm of happiness that God's holy words proclaim, but because the builder of a reign of justice, of love, and of peace is already in the midst of us . . .*

Octavio Duran

*Let us not be disheartened,*
>    *even when the horizon of history grows dim and closes in,*
*as though human realities made impossible*
*the accomplishment of God's plans.*
*God makes use even of human errors,*
>    *even of human sins,*
>    *so as to make rise over the darkness what Isaiah spoke of.*
*One day prophets will sing*
>    *not only the return from Babylon*
>    *but our full liberation.*
*"The people that walked in darkness have seen a great light.*
*They walk in lands of shadows,*
>    *but a light has shone forth."*

### Epiphany

*As the Magi from the East followed their star*
*and found Jesus,*
>    *who filled their hearts with boundless joy,*
*let us too,*
>    *even in hours of uncertainty, of shadows, of darkness*
>    *like those the Magi had,*
*not fail to follow that star,*
>    *the star of our faith . . .*

*Peace is not the product of terror or fear.*
*Peace is not the silence of the cemeteries.*
*Peace is not the silent result of violent repression.*
*Peace is the generous, tranquil contribution of all*
>    *to the good of all.*
*Peace is dynamism. Peace is generosity.*
*It is right and it is duty.*
*In it each one has a place in this beautiful family,*
*which the Epiphany brightens for us with God's light.*[135]

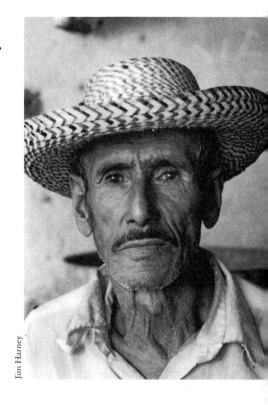

Jim Harney

# Human Rights

uman rights had become an important part of U.S. foreign policy, particularly during the presidency of Jimmy Carter (1976–1980). El Salvador, for that reason, became a point of contention in foreign policy debates, because the dual U.S. foreign policy goals of defeating communism and defending human rights were in conflict.[136]

Concerned about the attacks against the church for its defense of human rights, Georgetown University in Washington, DC, decided to offer Archbishop Romero an honorary degree in the humanities. What was unusual about the ceremony was that Romero did not travel to Washington to receive the award; the university traveled to San Salvador to present the award to Romero in the cathedral on February 14, 1978. The significance of this was not lost on Romero.

*There is something novel about this partly sacred, partly academic coming together of Georgetown University and our*

Romero delivers an address on receiving an honorary doctorate from Georgetown University. The honor was bestowed not in Washington but in the San Salvador Cathedral on February 14, 1978. (Arzobispado de San Salvador)

*cathedral. I am a pastor and teacher of the faith in this arch-diocese, and it is the university that comes to me, in my own cathedral, to confer on me its doctorate in humanities.*

*I wish to draw attention to the originality of this act as I express my gratitude and my welcome. This novel sign of a humble pastor, vested with the insignia of a university degree is, I believe, evocative of the prophetic and ecclesial dimension of the intentions both of Georgetown and of him who, filled with emotion and gratitude, receives this great honor.*[137]

Despite Romero's words of humility, and despite the fact that the apostolic delegate in Washington had called Georgetown University to see if the ceremony could be postponed, the award clearly recognized what so many others had already concluded, namely, that Romero was a true teacher. He taught with authority, because he lived what he taught. He proclaimed the Gospel and he lived it. He was, in a word, a credible witness to the Gospel.

Romero was gratified, above all, because the award expressed "solid support for that noble cause of Christian humanism that our church proclaims and defends."

*This service to human dignity that the church cannot renounce was raised by Paul VI to its highest theological level when he recalled: "In the countenance of every individual, especially in the countenance made transparent by tears and suffering, we can and should recognize the countenance of Christ . . . Our humanism becomes Christian; our Christianity becomes theocentric—so much so that we can also assert that, in order to know God, it is necessary to know human beings.*

*It was also a theological, transcendent perspective that inspired the Latin American bishops at Medellín when they directed the evangelization of our continent toward the service of human rights and the betterment of human beings. They felt it to be an authentic summons of the Spirit, one from which the church could not turn away: "a muted cry pours from the throats of millions . . . asking their pastors for a liberation that reaches them from nowhere else."*[138]

Romero further accepted the award as a recognition of all those who had collaborated in the cause of human rights: "I cannot accept this honor for myself alone. I feel that, in justice, I must share it with the whole of our local church—and also with those who, though not belonging to the church, have made this cause their own."

*"Georgetown's homage is a great satisfaction to us not only because, in itself, it is an honor, but above all because it is an acknowledgment of the authenticity of our cause: the cause of Christian humanism."*
—February 14, 1978

*"I share with all my brothers and sisters this honor that Georgetown has bestowed on us. It is a new voice of the Spirit which goes on pointing out to us the path that our church must follow."* —February 14, 1978

The award was also a concrete gesture of solidarity, "one that brings encouragement and hope to those who here suffer, in so many different and humiliating ways, from the violation of their fundamental rights." Citing the words of Paul VI from his 1965 address to the United Nations, Romero proclaimed:

*"We feel we are making our own the voice of the dead and the living," the Pope said on that occasion, speaking of the tragic consequences of war. Here we can think of the dead, victims of cruelty, and of those who continue to live, but in terror, under threat, bearing in their bodies the marks of torture, of outrages committed against them.*

*"We also make our own," the Pope went on, " the voice of the living who go forward confidently, the youth of the present generation, who legitimately expect a better human race. We also make our own the voice of the poor, the disinherited, the suffering, of those who long for justice, for a life with dignity for freedom, for well-being, and progress."*[139]

Romero concluded his address with a denunciation of violence, calling to conversion those who "assault and sacrifice the dignity of the images of God."

*Our church's service to, and defense of, human dignity, together with the sorrow and the shame of so many persons and of so many homes abused and left desolate has brought it to utter an anguished cry of denunciation and repudiation. "No to violence" it has cried out impartially against any hand raised against someone else, carrying out an act of violence that stains the world with sin.*[140]

Romero's address was greeted with enthusiastic applause by the people present. It was an affirmation of their hopes and dreams for an end to the violence and for justice. But the violence continued. Within a few weeks, Romero was lamenting "a week of bloodshed," this time in the rural areas surrounding the town of San Pedro Perulapán, just twelve miles east of San Salvador.

Two weeks of confrontations between peasants from FEC-CAS and UTC, who were protesting for access to agricultural credits, and the military, aided by the paramilitary group ORDEN, left 6 people dead, 68 missing, 14 wounded, peasant homes destroyed, and a continuing climate of fear.[141]

The day they searched the house was the worst. They

Religious News Service

took the men away captive, tied to each other like oxen. Their hands were tied behind their backs with mecate rope. Supposedly they were being taken prisoner, but they never came back, nor did anyone ever tell us where they were being taken, lined up like that, like animals.[142]

With the younger girls it was worse. After having them like that, tied up like iguanas, they did vulgar things to them. They stood in line for their turn, as though they were possessed by the devil, and they violated them, you know, in their private parts. One man after another raped them.[143]

On Easter Monday, Archbishop Romero opened the archdiocesan seminary, San José la Montaña, to receive the people who had been displaced from their homes by the repression. From that day on, the archdiocese continued to open its doors to persons who had been internally displaced and forced to seek protection from the church.

# Grassroots Organizations

Archbishop Romero's third pastoral letter, "The Church and Popular Political Organizations," was written in 1978, four months after the massacre of dozens of peasants at San Pedro Perulapán. For decades, these peasants had been denied access to land, exploited as seasonal labor in the coffee, sugarcane, and cotton harvests, and denied the right to organize in farmworker unions.

When they did organize, often with the encouragement of priests in the rural areas who were forming agricultural cooperatives and training peasants to become catechists, they joined campesino organizations such as FECCAS. Later, FECCAS merged with the UTC and joined teachers, students, and other sectors of the poor in a Popular Revolutionary Bloc to demand land and just salaries from the large landowners. Whenever they protested, they were subjected to arbitrary arrest, disappearance, torture, and assassination.

In this context, Romero took on directly the problem of popular political organizations and the problem of violence. He did

so in the spirit of *Octogesima Adveniens*,[144] as a local church seeking answers to concrete problems:

*Our pastoral letter quite deliberately offers no more than the Christian principles on which a solution must be based. It is a call for the whole people of God to reflect on these matters in local churches, in communion with the pastors and with the Universal Church, in the light of the Gospel, and in fidelity to the true identity of the Church.*[145]

Romero met for several sessions over breakfast with some fifteen priests, theologians, and political and economic analysts to prepare the letter, which went through four drafts. In the end, it was Romero who decided what would be said and how it would be said. It was published August 6, 1978, and was signed by both Romero and Bishop Rivera y Damas.[146]

*Medellín made it quite clear that, in the particular situation of Latin America, it is an "eminently Christian task" and, therefore, part of the "pastoral policy" of the Latin American hierarchy "to encourage and favor the efforts of the people to create and develop their own grassroots organizations for the redress and consolidation of their rights and the search for true justice."*[147]

Romero went further to identify "this proliferation of popular organizations as 'one of the signs of the times' that challenge the Church to exercise its power and duty of discernment and guidance in the light of the word of God that has been given to it to be applied to the problems of history."

One of the principles Romero states for this defense of popular organizations is "that the Church has a mission of service to the people."

*It is the role of the church to gather into itself all that is human in the people's cause and struggle, above all in the cause of the poor. The church identifies with the poor when they demand their legitimate rights. In our country the right they are demanding is hardly more than the right to survive, to escape from misery.*[148]

This solidarity with just aims is not restricted to Christian-based organizations:

*Whether they call themselves Christian or not, whether they are protected by the government, legally or in practice, or whether they are independent of it and opposed to it: if the*

> "On accepting the word of God, Christians find that it is a living word that brings with it awareness and demands. That is to say, it makes them aware of what sin and grace are, and of what must be resisted and what must be built up on earth. It is a word that demands of our consciences and of our lives not only that we judge the world by the criteria of the kingdom of God, but that we act accordingly. It is a word of God that we must not only hear but put into practice."
>
> —Third Pastoral Letter

*aim of the struggle is just, the Church will support it with all the power of the Gospel.*[149]

Nor is this defense of popular organizations only or primarily a political option, but a part of evangelization. Romero quotes Paul VI and *Evangelii Nuntiandi* to make this point:

*"It is the role of the church to gather into itself all that is human in the people's cause and struggle, above all in the cause of the poor. The church identifies with the poor when they demand their legitimate rights. In our country the right they are demanding is hardly more than the right to survive, to escape from misery."*

—Third Pastoral Letter

Peoples, as we know, are engaged with all their energy in the effort and struggle to overcome everything that condemns them to remain on the margin of life: famine, chronic disease, illiteracy, poverty, injustices in international relations and especially in commercial exchanges, situations of economic and cultural neo-colonialism, sometimes as cruel as the old political colonialism.

The Church, as the bishops repeated, has the duty to proclaim the liberation of millions of human beings, many of whom are its own children, the duty of assisting the birth of this liberation, of giving witness to it, of ensuring that it is complete. This is not foreign to evangelization.[150]

The practical implications of making a political option were outlined by Romero as follows:

*Faith and politics ought to be united in a Christian who has a political vocation, but they are not to be identified [as one] . . . Faith ought to inspire political action, not be mistaken for it.*[151]

The subject of violence is closely related to popular organizations. Poverty was a form of "institutional violence" that was deeply entrenched in El Salvador, and was itself the primary cause of the widening gap between rich and poor. The rich benefited from a concentration of land and wealth, while the poor continued to be exploited and to live in misery. This in turn led to a secondary violence between the rich and the poor, the rich resorting to violence through the army and the security forces to protect their land and their wealth, and the poor resorting, at times, to violence to defend their lives or to achieve their just demands.

Archbishop Romero used a threefold approach to analyze the violence, first distinguishing the different kinds of violence, then offering the church's moral judgment on each kind, and finally applying these judgments and teachings to the particular situation in El Salvador.

*The most acute form in which violence appears on our continent*

Romero enjoys a picnic with his driver and staff of the archdiocese.
(Octavio Duran)

*and in our own country is what the bishops of Medellín called "institutionalized violence." It is the result of an unjust situation in which the majority of men, women, and children in our country find themselves deprived of the necessities of life . . .*

*Alongside institutionalized violence there frequently arises "repressive violence," that is to say, the use of violence by the state security forces to contain the aspirations of the majority, violently crushing any signs of protest against the injustices we have mentioned.*[152]

Romero condemned both "institutionalized violence" and "repressive violence," and added "seditious or terrorist violence," and "spontaneous violence" to the list of illegitimate responses. The only kind of violence that is permissible, according to the church, is "violence in legitimate self-defense," but the church prefers "the constructive dynamism of non-violence." He concluded:

*The Christian is peaceful and not ashamed of it . . . He is not simply a pacifist, for he can fight, but prefers peace to war. The Christian knows that violent changes in structures would be fallacious, ineffectual in themselves, and not conforming to human dignity.*[153]

# Tear Off the Veil of Shame

The question of violence would not be resolved by a pastoral letter. The economic divisions in the country had deepened the resentment and hatred felt by rich and poor alike. Violent attacks, torture, disappearances, and assassinations had hardened those divisions into irreconcilable differences.

The peasants had not forgotten la matanza, the 1932 massacre of thirty thousand peasants in Izalco. The possibility of a social explosion, if not an organized rebellion, was not unthinkable. This, at least, was the assessment of Archbishop Romero.

*The peace in which we believe is, however, the fruit of justice . . . As a simple analysis of our structures shows and as history confirms, violent conflicts will not disappear until their underlying causes disappear . . . Further use of repressive violence will unhappily do nothing more than increase the conflict and make less hypothetical and more real the situation in which recourse to force, in legitimate self-defense, can be justified. We therefore regard as a most urgent task the establishment of social justice.*[154]

*"As pastor, I invite you to listen to the hoarse, imperfect echo of my words. But do not regard the instrument; regard the one who bids me tell you of God's infinite love. Be converted! Be reconciled! Love one another!"*

—March 16, 1980

Yet Romero continued to hold out hope, even to his last day, that justice could be established by peaceful means. Nowhere does this conviction stand forth more forcefully than in his preaching. He considered himself nothing more than "an ordinary catechist, an evangelizer of the people."[155]

*"Here on this mountain I will tear off the veil*
 *that enshrouds all peoples,*
 *the cloth that covers all nations.*
*Here the Lord will annihilate death forever.*
*Here God will wipe away the tears from every face,*
 *and his people's shame will depart from all the land."*
*Let us sing a song of hope*
*and be filled with cheerful spirit,*
*knowing that this Christian life,*
 *which came to us with Christ through the Virgin Mary*
 *and takes on flesh in all believers,*
*is the presence of God, who makes us a promise:*

*No, brothers and sisters,*
*El Salvador need not always live like this.*
*"I will tear off the veil of shame*
*    that covers it among all peoples.*
*I will wipe away the tears"*
*    of all those mothers who no longer have tears*
*    for having wept so much*
*    over their children who are not found.*
*Here too will he take away the sorrow*
*of all those homes that this Sunday suffer*
*    the mystery of dear ones abducted*
*    or suffer murder*
*    or torture*
*    or torment.*
*That is not of God.*
*God's banquet will come;*
*wait for the Lord's hour.*
*Let us have faith;*
*all this will pass away*
*    like a national nightmare,*
*and we shall awake to the Lord's great feast.*
*Let us be filled with this hope.*[156]

Octavio Duran

Romero had a keen sense of the Spirit of God working in history, and an unshakable conviction that history was guided by God's providence toward its eschatological end. That did not mean that everything that happened in history was God's will. On the contrary, human sinfulness and the stark reality of evil—murder, torture, torment—were obstacles to human flourishing and were not of God.

History was a drama, but the Lord's feast awaited those who live with faith. That was why Romero was filled with hope, and this hope allowed him to see the workings of the Spirit in history.

*There is a further connection, more fundamental and based on faith, between the church and popular organizations, even if they do not profess to be Christian. The church believes that the action of the Spirit who brings Christ to life in human beings is greater than itself. Far beyond the confines of the church, Christ's redemption is powerfully at work.*

*The strivings of individuals and groups, even if they do not profess to be Christian, derive their impetus from the Spirit of*

National Catholic Reporter

*Jesus. The church will try to see them in this way in order to purify them, encourage and incorporate them, together with the efforts of Christians, into the overall plan of Christian redemption.*[157]

This confidence was soon to be tested. On November 28, Father Ernesto "Neto" Barrera died in mysterious circumstances. The government claimed that he and three others died in a five-hour shoot-out with security forces. The Popular Liberation Forces, one of the guerrilla groups, claimed him as a revolutionary hero. Romero faced the immediate predicament: Should he preside at Barrera's funeral? Should Father Barrera be buried as a priest?[158]

The question of legitimate and illegitimate violence that his pastoral letter addressed returned, this time in the person of one of his priests. Could one resist with force the violence of repression, the denial of human rights, the institutionalized violence of unjust structures?[159]

He consulted with practically everybody. He always did,

but Neto's case was special. It was a tremendous challenge for him and for many of us as well.

"Don't go, Monseñor. They'll just use it against you."

"It should be a quiet burial."

"Just go and give your condolences to the family. Don't do anything else . . ."

"In order to make the decision I need to make, I'm just asking myself one question right now, just one."

We, who had arrived trembling, were even more frightened now. What would he ask us? If Neto had or hadn't joined the guerrillas? If he carried a weapon or not? If we . . .

"What I'm asking myself is this. What must Doña Marita, Neto's mother, be thinking now? Would it matter to her if Neto was carrying a weapon or not? If he was a guerrilla or not? Would she care? Neto was her son, and she was his mother, and so Doña Marita is there by his side now.

"The Church is also Neto's mother, and as a bishop I am his father. I should be by his side as well."[160]

Octavio Duran

Romero presided at Father Barrera's funeral and burial in his brother's parish in Mejicanos, a poor barrio of San Salvador. He had no knowledge of Barrera's political activities, nor did he approve of the use of violence. But he was Neto's bishop, and he would be there to bury his priest.

Romero's judgment on violence was clear:

*Even in legitimate cases, violence ought to be a last resort. All peaceful means must first be tried. We are living in explosive times and there is a great need for wisdom and serenity. We extend a fraternal invitation to all, but especially those organizations that are committed to the struggle for justice, to proceed courageously and honorably, always to maintain just objectives, and to make use of nonviolent means of persuasion rather than to put all their trust in violence.*[161]

# Christ Living among Us

## EXCERPTS FROM ROMERO'S HOMILIES

### First Sunday in Advent

*Everyone who struggles for justice,*
*everyone who makes just claims in unjust surroundings*
*is working for God's reign,*
    *even though not a Christian.*
*The church does not comprise all of God's reign;*
*God's reign goes beyond the church's boundaries.*

*The church values everything that is in tune*
    *with its struggle to set up God's reign.*
*A church that tries only to keep itself*
    *pure and uncontaminated*
*would not be a church of God's service to people.*
*The authentic church is one that does not mind*
*conversing with prostitutes and publicans and sinners,*
    *as Christ did—*

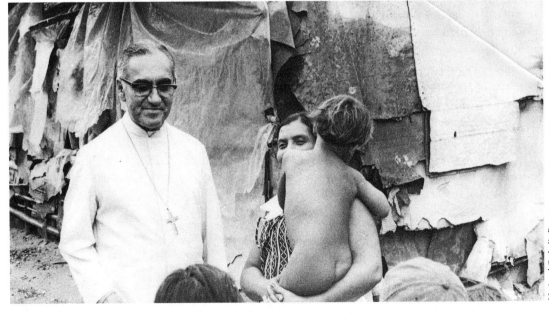

National Catholic Reporter

and with Marxists and those of various political movements—
in order to bring them salvation's true message . . .
Some want to keep a gospel so disembodied
    that it doesn't get involved at all
    in the world it must save.
Christ is now in history.
Christ is in the womb of the people.
Christ is now bringing about
    the new heavens and the new earth . . .

Advent should admonish us to discover
in each brother or sister that we greet,
in each friend whose hand we shake,
in each beggar who asks for bread,
in each worker who wants to use the right to join a union,
in each peasant who looks for work in the coffee groves,
    the face of Christ.
Then it would not be possible to rob them,
    to cheat them,
    to deny them their rights.
They are Christ,
and whatever is done to them
Christ will take as done to himself.
This is what Advent is:
    Christ living among us.

## Second Sunday in Advent

God comes, and his ways are near to us.
God saves in history.
Each person's life, each one's history,
    is the meeting place God comes to.
How satisfying to know one need not go to the desert
    to meet him,
need not go to some particular spot in the world.
God is in your own heart . . .

Who will put a prophet's eloquence into my words
to shake from their inertia
all those who kneel before the riches of the earth—
who would like gold, money, lands, power, political life

Scott Wright

85

*to be their everlasting gods?*
*All that is going to end.*
*There will remain only the satisfaction of having been,*
> *in regard to money or political life,*
> *a person faithful to God's will.*
*One must learn to manage the relative and transitory*
> *things of earth according to his will,*
> *not make them absolutes.*
*There is only one absolute: he who awaits us*
> *in the heaven that will not pass away.*

### Third Sunday in Advent

*I invite you this week, in this hour*
> *when El Salvador seems to have no place for joy,*
*to listen to St. Paul repeat to us:*
> *"Be always joyful.*
> *Be constant in prayer.*
> *In every circumstance give thanks.*
> *This is God's will for you in Christ Jesus."*
*The Christian, the Christian community, must not despair.*
*If someone dies in the family,*
> *we must not weep like people without hope.*
*If the skies have darkened in our nation's history,*
> *let us not lose hope.*
*We are a community of hope,*
*and like the Israelites in Babylon,*
> *let us hope for the hour of liberation.*
*It will come.*
> *It will come because God is faithful, says St. Paul.*
*This joy must be like a prayer.*
*"He who called you is faithful,"*
> *and he will keep his promises . . .*

*If Christ had become incarnate now*
> *and were a thirty-year-old man today,*
*he could be here in the cathedral*
> *and we wouldn't know him from the rest of you—*
*a thirty-year-old man, a peasant from Nazareth,*
> *here in the cathedral like any peasant*
> *from our countryside.*

*The Son of God made flesh would be here*
*and we wouldn't know him—*
*one completely like us . . .*

**Fourth Sunday in Advent**

*God keeps on saving in history.*
*And so, in turning once again*
*to the episode of Christ's birth at Bethlehem,*
*we come not to recall Christ's birth twenty centuries ago,*
*but to live that birth here,*
*in the twentieth century, this year,*
*in our own Christmas here in El Salvador.*
*By the light of these Bible readings*
*we must continue all the history*
*that God has in his eternal mind,*
*even to the concrete events*
*of our abductions,*
*of our tortures,*
*of our own sad history.*
*That is where we are to find our God . . .*
*No one can celebrate a genuine Christmas*
*Without being truly poor.*
*The self-sufficient,*
*the proud,*
*those who, because they have everything,*
*look down on others,*
*those who have no need even of God—*
*for them there will be no Christmas.*
*Only the poor,*
*the hungry,*
*those who need someone to come on their behalf,*
*will have that someone.*
*That someone is God,*
*Emmanuel,*
*God-with-us.*
*Without poverty of spirit*
*there can be no abundance of God.*

**Christmas**

*Christ put his classroom of redemption*

Steve Moriarity

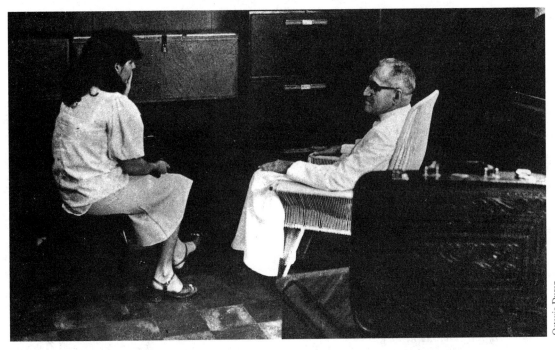

Octavio Duran

*among the poor—*
*not because money is evil,*
*but because money often makes slaves*
    *of those who worship the things of earth*
    *and forget about God.*

### Epiphany

*God's reign must be established now on earth. That reign of God finds itself hindered, manacled, by many idolatrous misuses of money and power. Those false gods must be overthrown, just as the first evangelizers in the Americas overthrew the false goods that our natives adored. Today the idols are different. They are called money, they are called political interests, they are called national security. As idolatries, they are trying to displace God from his altar. The church declares that people can be happy only when, like the Magi, they adore the one true God . . .*

*My position as pastor obliges me to solidarity*
    *with everyone who suffers*
*and to embody*
    *every effort for human freedom and dignity.*[162]

# Octavio, My Son

On the night of January 19, 1979, Father Octavio Ortiz was leading a "young people's Christian initiation gathering" in the El Despertár retreat center run by the San Antonio Abad parish in San Salvador. Thirty young men, most of them teenagers, were in attendance. Octavio began the retreat with a reflection on Jesus' sermon in the synagogue in Nazareth: "What does it mean to give sight to the blind?" "What does it mean to free the oppressed?"

The following morning, at 6:00 a.m., a military tank broke down the gate to the retreat center, and bullets were flying. "Crush him! Kill him!" the soldiers shouted. In five minutes, the military operation was over. Octavio's body was lying on the patio in a puddle of blood, his face smashed by the tank. Another four bodies were riddled with bullets from the machine gun fire. Later, the soldiers rearranged the bodies and placed pistols in their hands to make it look like a shoot-out.[163]

Later that day, Archbishop Romero arrived at the morgue, wracked with sorrow. The entrance was totally militarized. Father Octavio was the first priest Romero ordained after becoming a bishop. Now he was dead.

*"Christ invites us not to fear persecution. Believe me, brothers and sisters, anyone committed to the poor must risk the same fate as the poor. And in El Salvador we know what the fate of the poor signifies: to disappear, to be tortured, to be captive, and to be found dead."*

*—February 17, 1970*

The floor was one big puddle of blood. The five of them were there thrown on the floor. Streams of blood were still coming out of them. Around them were some of the people in the community that had arrived before us.

"Where is Octavio?"

"Here, Monseñor. This is him." They pointed to him. You couldn't tell it was him. His body was completely flattened, his face destroyed to the point that it looked like he didn't even have one . . .

Monseñor Romero knelt on the ground and held his shattered head . . . Tears streamed from Monseñor's face as he held him close with all of his affection.

"They ran over him with a tank and smashed his head, Monseñor . . ."

The guardsmen looked in through the door. Monseñor's cassock was covered with blood and he was crying, cradling Father Octavio in his arms.

"Octavio, my son, you have completed your mission. You were faithful . . ."[164]

*"It is very easy to be servants of the word without disturbing the world: a very spiritualized word, a word without any commitment to history, a word that can sound in any part of the world because it belongs to no part of the world. A word like that creates no problems, starts no problems.*

*What starts conflicts and persecutions, what marks the genuine church, is the word that, burning like the word of the prophets, proclaims and accuses . . . This is the hard service of the word. But God's Spirit goes with the prophet, with the preacher, for he is Christ, who keeps on proclaiming his reign to the people of all times."*

—December 10, 1977

The same morning that Octavio was killed, his father Alejandro was leaving the village where he grew up near Cacaopera, Morazan, some four hours to the east of San Salvador. Don Alejandro had met Romero in 1952, when Romero was a parish priest in San Miguel. It was Romero who gave Alejandro the Bible that he read together with his friends and family.

Octavio was the second of my 12 children. He wove hammocks and planted corn with us until one day, when he was 13 years old, he left the nest to fly on his own. He decided to go to the seminary in San Miguel where Father Romero was in charge of the boys that wanted to be priests.

When he reached that goal, and I saw my son lying prostrate on the floor in front of the bishop, face down, like they do in the ordination ceremonies for priests, I told Exaltación, my wife:

"He's going to be a priest, but he looks like he's dead."

When they killed him, I saw him lying prostrate again, and I said to myself:

"I saw him like this before, and now I'm seeing him again in the same way."

These are the mysteries that life holds.[165]

Don Alejandro had gone to San Salvador to give his son Octavio a message from his mother: "Tell Octavio to set aside a day to go to Esquipulas and see *El Cristo Negro*," the Black Christ. Before he arrived, however, he heard on the radio that his son had been assassinated. When he reached the cathedral in San Salvador, it was already night, and the five bodies were there. Archbishop Romero was discussing with people from Octavio's parish in Mejicanos where Octavio should be buried.

Monseñor Romero began. "We would like to have Octavio buried here in the cathedral as a martyr."

José Lavanderos

It didn't seem like a bad idea to me.

"But what do you think?" Monseñor asked me. "Shall we keep him here, or do you want to take him to your village to the cemetery there?"

Octavio was the only priest to have come out of Cacaopera. I think he was the only one from the whole department of Morazan. It didn't seem like a bad idea to bury him there in the land where he was born, in the land where his umbilical cord was buried.

"I don't know, Monseñor. I don't want to decide without talking to his mother. We need to think about it."

At that point, the people from the base communities indicated their unhappiness with the two options. It was as if they had already thought it out and decided.

"Octavio was with us in life, and he should stay here with us now!"[166]

And that's how Octavio came to be buried behind the altar of his parish, San Francisco Mejicanos, in San Salvador. On the stone slab in the pavement that marks his burial site are the two questions that he asked the young people at the retreat, the night before he was killed: "What does it mean to give sight to the blind?" "What does it mean to free the oppressed?" His father added:

Life holds such mysteries, and God has us walk along such

Octavio Duran

*"The guarantee of one's prayer is not in saying a lot of words. The guarantee of one's petition is very easy to know: how do I treat the poor? Because that is where God is."*

—February 5, 1978

unforeseeable paths! He was the first of my sons to be killed. They killed all of them later. Angel in 1980, Santos Angel and Jesus in 1985 and Ignacio in 1990. So in the struggle for our people, I lost all of my sons. The ones I have left are my daughters and my grandchildren. We've named one of the little ones Octavio, thinking that maybe this little Tavito will grow up to be a priest someday.[167]

More than a hundred priests gathered for the funeral Mass in the cathedral the next morning. Archbishop Romero asked priests to cancel other Masses so that they could concelebrate with him: "This is a murder that speaks to us of resurrection," he began. "Christ calls us to conversion . . . and to be that light of the world, that salt and light of the earth, we must believe."[168]

He also denounced the security forces and the government for the assassinations, and for covering up what had happened: "We no longer believe in the justice and the truth found in our own surroundings." Romero then mentioned statements made by General Romero to the effect that "there isn't any persecution of the church." The best response to that statement, the archbishop said, is the bodies of the priest and the four youths.

# Puebla

The day after he buried Father Octavio Ortiz, Archbishop Romero left for the Latin American Bishops' Conference in Puebla, Mexico. In his funeral homily Romero had observed: "The conflict is not between the church and the government; it is between the government and the people. The church is with the people and the people are with the church, thanks be to God!" People applauded.[169]

By now, Romero was known throughout the world as a vocal defender of human rights and social justice. Along with Hélder Câmara from Brazil and Leonidas Proaño from Ecuador, he was one of the bishops most featured in the Mexican press. Nevertheless, Romero did not take a leading part in the conference but worked quietly on the commission on evangelization and human development. "He was a country pastor at heart, shy, direct, and simple, like a campesino."[170]

Romero did, however, give a series of press conferences in the evening to standing room only audiences. He shared with people the tragic events that had transpired in El Salvador, including the assassination of Father Octavio Ortiz just two days before his arrival in Puebla.

When asked about his supposed conversion through his contact with the poor and persecuted, he responded, "Would that I were converted!" evoking laughter from the audience. He admitted that the events of the preceding two years had changed him, but he did not see the change as a radical break from his past.[171] "To be converted is to return to the true God and, in this sense, I feel that my contact with the poor, with those in need, brings me to feel even more my need for God."[172]

Romero made only one intervention in the assembly of bishops to give his recommendations for the final document:

*I believe that our document will not reflect all the gospel commitment that the church ought to take on so as not to lose its credibility in our lands if it does not emphasize an evangelization that effectively responds to the unjust distribution of wealth that God has created for all, and the noble longing of*

Archbishop Romero in Mexico City.
(Libro Reseña biográfica de Monseñor Romero, de J.P/ Jiménez y M. Navarrete)

all to associate freely and participate actively in the politics of the common good of their country.

It should be an evangelization that denounces with candor arbitrary arrest, political exile, torture, and above all the sorrowful mystery of the disappeared . . .

I believe too that our pastoral vision of reality would not be complete if it ignored and did not evangelically encourage new phenomena like our campesinos' efforts to organize, at times merely in order not to die of hunger.

It should note especially the heroic deaths of our priests and pastoral workers, all the more heroic in that slanderous official declarations try to discredit their work of awakening evangelical consciousness in the community.[173]

*"How sad it would be, in a country where such horrible murders are being committed, if there were no priests among the victims! They are the testimony of a church incarnated in the problems of its people."*

Romero shared one memorable evening with several bishops who shared his commitment to the poor, along with many liberation theologians and social scientists, most of them priests, who were advising these same bishops at the conference. Out of the evening came a letter, signed by those present, in support of human rights in El Salvador. "Dear Brother," the letter began:

We encourage you to continue on this narrow and steep way of building permanently the kingdom that Jesus Christ presents to his church as the gift of the Spirit and as its mission. With you we pray the Our Father, sharing together the bread of our commitment and of our hope. And the hope of the poor will not perish, for theirs is the promise.[174]

When Romero returned to El Salvador, he was greeted by a large reception at the airport and a crowded Mass at the cathedral. There he highlighted some of the key themes of Puebla, including the "preferential option for the poor" and the "social mortgage on private property."

Soon after, the Salvadoran bishops took the official copy of the Puebla document to San Miguel to lay at the feet of El Salvador's patron saint, Our Lady of Peace, so that she could give them her blessing. Eighty priests, several nuns, and people from the basic Christian communities accompanied Romero and greeted him after Mass with a cry: *"Viva Monseñor Romero! Viva!"*[175]

Romero returned from Puebla renewed and encouraged by

the warm reception and support that he had received from other bishops and from people around the world. This sense of renewal was reflected in the confidence with which he preached, and the hope that he radiated:

With his seminarians. (Octavio Duran)

*I have often been asked here in El Salvador: What can we do? Is there no way out of this situation in El Salvador? And filled with hope and with faith, not only divine faith but human faith, believing also in human beings, I say: Yes, there is a way out! Let those exits not be closed off . . .*

*You have the key to the solution. But the church gives you what you cannot have by yourselves: hope, the optimism to struggle, the joy of knowing that there is a solution, that God is our Father and keeps on urging us. He needed people to take the paralytic up to the roof and lower him before Christ so that he could cure him.*

*Christ and God could bring about by themselves our people's salvation, but they want also to have stretcher-bearers, people to help pick up that paralytic called the nation or society—so that with human hands, with human solutions, with human ideas, we can put him down before Christ, who is the only one who can say, "I have seen your faith. Get up and walk." And I believe that our people will get up and will walk."* [176]

Octavio Duran

This renewed confidence and hope, however, would soon be checked by the chilly reception he would receive in Rome. In May, Romero decided to consult with the new pope, John Paul II. It would be their first face-to-face meeting. In preparation for the visit, Romero shared with the people of El Salvador what he would say: "Holy Father . . . know that I have preached the Gospel and I am ready to keep on preaching that Gospel of the Lord in defense of the beloved people that the Lord has entrusted to me." [177]

The meeting, which took place on May 7, was difficult, but frank. Romero showed the pope a picture of Octavio's crushed face: "I knew Octavio very well, Holy Father." The pope sat quietly, but unmoved. His message, which he repeated several times to Romero during the meeting, was clear: "Make efforts to have a better relationship with your country's government," he emphasized. It was a crushing blow for Romero.[178]

Upon his return, Romero was once again greeted by the downward spiral of violence. On May 8, 1979, security forces opened fire on protesters who had occupied the cathedral and who were standing on the front steps. Twenty-five were killed and seventy-five were wounded in a dramatic scene captured on film by several foreign television channels and broadcast around the world.[179]

# Church in the Midst of Crisis

Violence continued throughout the end of May and the beginning of June 1979. Protesters continued to occupy churches and embassies. The security forces responded by violently attacking the protesters. Finally, the government imposed a state of siege. Teachers, labor union leaders, peasants and political leaders were targeted by right-wing groups and paramilitary death squads.

On June 20, Father Rafael Palacios was shot down in the streets of Santa Tecla, in reprisal for the killing of a military officer. He became the fifth priest to be assassinated in El Salvador. Once again Romero invited other priests to cancel their Masses and to concelebrate the funeral Mass in the cathedral with him.

In his homily, Romero said that Father Rafael was a victim "of the structural sin built into, and embedded in our society." His message, however, was one of hope: "Father Rafael always believed more in the force of love than in the force of violence . . . His ideal was to create communities inspired by the love of Jesus Christ." His death, however, had an additional significance:

> We can present along with the blood of teachers, of laborers, of peasants, the blood of our priests. This is a communion of love. It would be sad, if in a country where murder is being committed so horribly, we were not to find priests also among the victims. They are the testimony of a church incarnated in the problems of its people.[180]

On August 4, a sixth priest was killed in his parish in San Esteban Catarina, in the department of San Vicente. Napoleón Alirio Macías was assassinated between the sacristy and the altar by three National Guardsmen in civilian dress. Romero attended his funeral Mass on August 6, the feast of the Transfiguration, the same day that he published his fourth pastoral letter.[181]

Archbishop Romero's final pastoral letter, "The Church's Mission amid the National Crisis," written August 6, 1979, took his analysis of popular political organizations and violence one step further as he first analyzed, then judged in light of the Gospel and Catholic social teaching, the political projects in

Martyred priests, Fathers Rafael Palacios and Napoleón Alirio Macías. (Courtesy Maryknoll Archives)

Octavio Duran

conflict in El Salvador, relying on the conclusions reached by the bishops in Puebla.

In addition, Romero consulted the priests and basic Christian communities of his archdiocese about crucial questions affecting both the church and Salvadoran society. He asked them: "Who is Jesus Christ for you?" "What is our country's greatest sin?" "What do you think about the bishops' conference, the nuncio, the archbishop?" According to Jon Sobrino, he took their responses to heart.

> Monseñor taught with authority, but not with exclusivity; he offered his teaching with firmness, but not as a mere formal imposition. His writings were the fruit of reflection on the problems of the poor and in dialogue with them. For that reason, there was an evolution in his teaching.
>
> Monseñor Romero taught, and all the while he was learning, consulting with others and allowing himself to be challenged by the anguish and hope of the poor. His magisterium tried to illuminate social and political problems from the specific standpoint of the church; this historical reality, at the same time, shed light on what should be the pastoral activity of the church.[182]

Romero cites Paul VI and *Octogesima Adveniens* as the starting point for his pastoral letter:

> The Holy People of God shares also in Christ's prophetic office . . . under the guidance of sacred teaching authority . . . With the help of the Holy Spirit . . . and in dialogue with other Christians and all men and women of good will, the people discern the options and commitments that are called for in order to bring about the social, political and economic changes seen in many cases to be urgently needed.[183]

Like the Puebla documents, Romero begins with an analysis of the social, economic, and political reality in El Salvador, then looks at that reality in the light of the church's teaching and mission, and finally determines the pastoral implications for the church. In addition, Romero takes a more critical look at violence and Marxism, distinguishing and judging different expressions of each.

Romero begins with the recognition of the deepening crisis of the poor, which occurred during the ten years between Medellín and Puebla. That "muted cry" of wretchedness that Medellín heard ten years before, Puebla describes as "loud and clear, increasing in violence and intensity."[184]

> This situation of pervasive extreme poverty takes on very concrete faces in real life. In these faces, we ought to recognize the suffering features of Christ the Lord, who questions and challenges us. They include: the faces of young children, struck down by poverty before they are born . . . the faces of young people who are disoriented because they cannot find their place in society . . . the faces of indigenous people and Afro-Americans . . . the faces of peasants deprived of land . . . the faces of laborers who have difficulty organizing and defending their rights . . . the faces of the unemployed . . . the faces of the marginalized . . . the faces of old people.[185]

He then analyzes the root causes of these manifestations of social injustice in a profounder way than he had done in his previous pastoral letters, condemning the absolutization of capitalism and national security as concrete idols that cause the poor to die a slow death due to conditions of poverty and misery, or a quick death due to military repression:

> *All of this explains the firm opposition of important sectors of capital to initiatives, whether of the people or of the government, that, through trade union organizations, seek to improve the living conditions, or to raise the wages of the working class. The ruling class, especially the rural elite, cannot allow unions to be organized among either rural or urban laborers so long as, from a capitalist point of view, they believe their economic interests are at risk. This viewpoint makes repression against popular organizations something necessary in order to maintain and increase profit levels, even though it is at the cost of the growing poverty of the working class . . .* [186]

*"More and more Salvadorans are learning the point that the deepest root of the serious evils that afflict us . . . is this 'structural violence.' It takes concrete form in the unjust distribution of wealth and of property . . . and in that amalgam of economic and political structures by which the few grow increasingly rich and powerful while the remainder grow increasingly poor and weak."*

—Fourth Pastoral Letter

*"The church is [Christ's] 'body in history.' We shall be more the church, and offer a better specific contribution from the church for the liberation of our people, the more we identify ourselves with him, and the more we are docile instruments of his truth and his grace."*

—Fourth Pastoral Letter

*This is the right place to draw attention also to the ideology that underlies this unjust repression. I am speaking of the "ideology of national security," which the Puebla document firmly denounces on many occasions. This new political theory and practice lies at the root of this situation of repression and of repressive violence against the most basic rights of the Salvadoran people.[187]*

The church, whose mission is to proclaim the Kingdom of God, must engage in "denouncing every lie, every injustice, and every sin that destroys God's plan." For that reason, the church is called to be . . .

*the voice of the voiceless, a defender of the rights of the poor, a promoter of every just aspiration for liberation, a guide, an empowerer, a humanizer of every legitimate struggle to achieve a more just society, a society that prepares the way for the true Kingdom of God in history.*

*This demands of the Church a greater presence among the poor. It ought to be in solidarity with them, running the risks they run, enduring the persecution that is their fate, ready to give the greatest possible testimony to its love by defending and promoting those who were first in Jesus' love.[188]*

But for this just society to be realized, profound structural changes must take place.

*To preach and to encourage the urgent need for profound structural changes in the social and political life of our country is another contribution that the pastoral mission of the Church can make . . . The full liberation of the Salvadoran people, not to mention personal conversions, demands a thorough change in the social, political, and economic system.[189]*

Who will bring about these profound transformations in Salvadoran society? It must be the poor themselves, and the church will be present to these changes to the degree that the poor are integrated into basic Christian communities. These communities "embody the Church's preferential love for the common people . . . and they are given a concrete opportunity to share in the task of the Church and to work . . . for the transformation of the world."[190]

# Pastoral Accompaniment

As the situation in El Salvador continued to grow tenser, a popular insurrection in Nicaragua resulted in the overthrow of the Somoza dictatorship and the victory of the Sandinista Revolution. In his Sunday homily after the July 19, 1979, victory, Romero offered his greeting to the people of Nicaragua.

> *I believe I interpret the feeling of all of you if our first greeting this morning is for our sister republic of Nicaragua. I salute it in a sense of fraternal prayer and solidarity, because today more than ever it needs that spiritual support . . . Over twenty-five thousand dead are not a trivial matter; the gift of God offered at this moment is not to be cast away.*[191]

Equipo Maíz

Nicaragua provided Romero with a backdrop from which to view the deteriorating situation in El Salvador. The bloodbath in Nicaragua showed what happens when power is made an absolute, Romero said, but it also showed that power could not be sustained by repression: "There comes a moment when the people tire of being exploited and oppressed"—at this point people in the cathedral burst into applause—"a wonderful lesson for those who believe in that force which cannot be maintained."[192]

In his August 6, 1979, pastoral letter, Romero reflected on the special challenges presented by the Nicaraguan revolution and the increasingly revolutionary situation in El Salvador. In particular, he examined the question of violence and Marxism, as he had done in previous pastoral letters.

With regard to violence, he cited the church's teaching about the right of legitimate defense, including insurrection, but cautioned against its use: "We know how cruel and painful the price of blood, and how hard to repair are the social and economic damages of war." With regard to Marxism, he distinguished between Marxism as an ideology, which he condemned, and Marxism as a method of social analysis which, when used correctly, is permissible.

What was new in this pastoral letter was his proposal for a

pastoral ministry of accompaniment, by which he meant offering orientation to those Christians who feel called to a vocation of political activism in a popular organization or political—even revolutionary—party.

> *The church cannot abandon Christians who, moved by good faith in their understanding of the Gospel, wish to participate in a political party or organization. We must follow them, but according to the church's way, following as pastors, so that these Christians may know that wherever they go they carry the germ, the word, the seed of salvation, the light of the Gospel.*[193]

Romero defined pastoral accompaniment as the ministry of evangelizing those "who have made a political option that they conscientiously see as their faith commitment in history." He was not speaking of "a politicized pastoral activity" but rather "a type of pastoral work that guides Christian consciences according to the Gospel in a politicized environment."[194] He had in mind the kind of orientation needed for committed Christians who were active in basic Christian communities, popular organizations, and political parties.

Romero had become increasingly aware of these challenges through his contact and dialogue with organized sectors of peasants, workers, and students who were leaders in their popular organizations and political parties. One such person was Apolinario "Polin" Serrano, a leader of FECCAS, one of the peasant unions, who had dialogued with Romero on numerous occasions and won his respect. One of Romero's biographers writes:

> Romero discovered the Christian roots of the popular and revolutionary commitment of those people. From this he discovered quite clearly that the revolution of these leftists drew its life much more from Christian teaching and ideals than from Marxist or communist ideology.[195]

Increasingly, Romero himself had begun to share the same indignities and harassment that the poor in the rural communi-

Romero visits the town of San Antonio los Ranchos in Chalatenango. (Octavio Duran)

ties had suffered. On the Sunday after the triumph of the Nicaraguan revolution, he recalled the pastoral visit he had made to rural villages in the department of Chalatenango the previous day.

> *Yesterday I was at San Miguel de Mercedes, simply doing my duty of encouraging the Christian communities that are fostered there. The military posted at either end of the town kept many people out and made them go back. They made me get out of the car too, and they searched it. They even suspect the bishop. And afterward they said it was for my security. If it was for my security, I thought, why are they suspicious about where I'm going when I'm seated here? And I said to them, "Why don't you let those people that you have stopped go in with me? I'll walk in with them." They were women; the guards wouldn't let them enter. Afterward I had the chance to meet the people at San Antonio Los Ranchos—they were there waiting for me, because they were very eager to converse with their pastor.*[196]

Twice more in August, Romero was subject to harassment by the military during his pastoral visits to Chalatenango. On both occasions, the military forced him to get out of his car.

We were waiting for Monseñor in Arcatao at 7:30 in the morning. But at around 7:00, nine truckloads of soldiers

Octavio Duran

came from Chalatenango and militarized our whole town . . . When Monseñor's little car got to the river, they stopped it and made him get out. The priests and nuns traveling with him had to get out, too.

"Get out! We have to search this vehicle!" "Search as much as you want," Monseñor told them, "but you're not going to find what you're looking for."

They went through everything: the floor of the car, the seats, the seat linings. They opened up the hood to look at the motor . . . Then they looked in the trunk. They took some of his letters out of the glove compartment, opened them up and read them . . . Everything they did, they did to bother him. Finally they let him go. We followed along walking beside the car, but when it got to the center of Arcatao, the soldiers stopped him again. This time, they were even worse.

"Everybody out! Put your hands on the car!"

There they searched each one of them individually. They touched Monseñor all over his body, without any respect for him. They lifted his cassock. They tried to humiliate him, frisking him as if he were a criminal, and when they were done, one of the guardsmen said mockingly:

"This is all for your protection. We have orders to protect you!"

"You should be protecting the people," he said calmly.

When we finally got Monseñor to ourselves, we gave him a warm welcome to help him forget about the insulting way he'd been treated. The soldiers were . . . enraged.[197]

The Mass was kept under surveillance and tape-recorded by the military, but the people were not afraid. "Go ahead and kill us now, why don't you? We don't care as long as we're with Monseñor!"

# October Crisis

From January to September 1979, 65 people had been disappeared, and 580 people had been murdered in El Salvador—four times more than the previous year. "The government has emptied the prisons of political prisoners," Romero commented, "but unfortunately the cemeteries have been filled with the dead."

On September 29, Romero suffered a personal loss when his friend Apolinario Serrano, and three other peasant leaders, were killed by soldiers at a military roadblock. Friends recall seeing Romero, his face turned toward the wall.

Archbishop Romero with his auxiliary bishop Arturo Rivera y Damas.
(Octavio Duran)

> He can't lie down. He can't erase him from his memory. He can't even pray . . . They took him away from the people. And Monseñor Romero is crying for him. He covers his face, and remembers him the way he was when he was alive.[198]

The following Sunday, Romero recalled his friend with affection.

> *He was a man much loved, of great hope for achieving justice for the peasantry. I believe one of the gravest errors and one of the injustices that most cry to heaven has been committed. The people are deprived of their hopes and of the voices that denounce their oppression.*[199]

With every day, the country was edging toward civil war. Archbishop Romero had already received a secret visit from a military officer informing him of a plan to replace General Romero and to form a new government. On October 7, two military officials confirmed the plan. Three days later Archbishop Romero met with two of his advisers to discuss what posture the church should take in the event of a military coup. On October 15, the bloodless coup took place and General Romero left the country for Guatemala.

The coup took the popular organizations by surprise, particularly since the new government included Roman Mayorga, the president of the Central American University, and Guillermo Ungo, a leading figure of the political opposition, as well as a leader of the business community and two military officers. Archbishop Romero at first gave cautious support to the new government and indicated his willingness to dialogue and collaborate. But he met fierce criticism from within his own church:

Octavio Duran

> They're still killing, and they're still stealing, and he's still supporting them? In Zacamil we were really angry with Monseñor Romero because of his sympathy for the junta . . .
>
> "You're putting too much trust in those people!"
>
> "And they're the same old military people as always. Look at all of them in the same position they've always been in. Everyone knows the crimes they've committed! They talked about purging people from the military, but who have they purged? No one!"
>
> "You're going to see how the military people are controlling the civilian friends of yours in the government. You'll see, Monseñor . . ."
>
> "You can't let yourself be deceived, Monseñor, and you can't go on deceiving the people!"
>
> He listened to us patiently for a while, but then he got angry.[200]

Protests continued in the streets, and seventy persons were killed when security forces attacked a demonstration. Romero was called upon to secure the protection of six hundred people who had taken refuge in El Rosario Church, and the release of a police officer held captive by the demonstrators. The violence subsided, but only temporarily.

On December 10, the new government announced plans for a new land reform: 40 percent of the land in El Salvador was held by less than 1 percent of the population. Seventy-three percent of the rural children were undernourished, 67 percent of rural women gave birth without medical assistance, and only 37 percent of rural families had access to springs of water.[201] Romero welcomed the announcement, but already he was beginning to distance himself from the junta.

In his homily on Christmas eve, Romero called for hope.

*The country is giving birth to a new age, and therefore there are pain and anguish, blood and suffering. But as in childbirth, says Christ, the woman whose hour has come suffers, but when the new child has been born she then forgets all her pains. These sufferings will pass. Our joy will be that in this hour of childbirth we were Christians, that we lived clinging to faith in Christ, that pessimism did not overcome us. How I would like to cry out over all the fields of El Salvador this night the angels' great news: Fear not! A Savior is born! What now seems insoluble, a dead end, God is already marking with a hope.*[202]

But while Romero's Christian hope was real, his hope in the new government had all but disappeared by the end of the year. On December 26, the military high command called the civilian members of the junta to a meeting and bluntly told them that the civilians were in the government at the military's pleasure.

On December 30, a majority of the civilians in the new government sent a letter to the military high command informing them of their intention to resign unless there were an end to the growing wave of repression against the people. They called on Romero to mediate the conflict as a last measure to hold the government together.

During the last days of the year, Romero received comfort from the visit of Cardinal Aloisio Lorscheider, an important leader of the Brazilian church, who arrived in San Salvador to make a brief visit. Though he was on a mission on behalf of the Holy See, he and Romero shared the same vision for the church. Romero said, "I feel in the visit of this new envoy of the pope a further confirmation of the work our archdiocese is doing."[203]

Subsequently, Cardinal Lorscheider told one of Romero's biographers:

I saw how much Archbishop Romero was committed to his people, and the force and authenticity of his witness. He was a true shepherd who was ready to give his life for his sheep—which is what happened, as could well be foreseen.[204]

*"Because it is God's work, we don't fear the prophetic mission the Lord has entrusted to us. I can imagine someone saying, 'So now he thinks he's a prophet!' No, it's not that I think I'm a prophet; it's that you and I are a prophetic people. Everyone baptized has received a share in Christ's prophetic mission."* —July 8, 1979

# A New Ray of Salvation

Fr. D. Bank

Scott Wright

### Second Sunday in Advent

*Historical moments will change,*
*    but God's design will ever be the same:*
*to save human beings in history.*
*Therefore, the church,*
*entrusted with carrying out God's design,*
*cannot be identified with any historical design.*
*The church could not be the ally of the Roman Empire*
*or of Herod*
*    or of any king on earth*
*    or of any political system*
*    or of any human political strategy.*
*It will enlighten them all*
*but it will always remain authentically*
*    the one that proclaims salvation history,*
*    God's design.*

### Third Sunday in Advent

*Let's not forget, dear Christians,*
*    that the church was born of sinners.*
*The church is holy, because it has God's Spirit*
*    giving it life;*
*but it is sinful and it needs conversion,*
*    because we make it up—humans tending toward evil*
*and at times perhaps with a past that shames us.*

*But once we are converted,*
*    we try—we try!*
*    to follow the Lord.*
*We don't follow him as yet with perfection,*
*but the effort to follow him*
*is what makes a true disciple of our Lord Jesus Christ.*

Octavio Duran

### Fourth Sunday in Advent

*The salvation we preach in Christ's church is the same
salvation that Mary believed in and that she initiated when she
gave her consent and became fruitful with God's salvation. The
church is zealous to guard Mary's belief, God's plan for human
salvation, and it will not let his plan be lost in merely human
plans. Rather, it must sanctify and permeate these. Every
people's liberation effort will be effective and according to
God's heart only if it lets faith in God's plan to save humanity
pervade it.*

### Christmas

*We must not seek the child Jesus
        in the pretty figures of our Christmas cribs.
We must seek him among the undernourished children
        who have gone to bed tonight with nothing to eat,
        among the poor newsboys
        who will sleep covered with newspapers in doorways.*

### Epiphany

*Is there no longer any hope?
What will happen to the agrarian reform . . . ?
What will happen to the famous abolition of the death squads . . . ?*

Octavio Duran

*What will happen with the problem of the disappeared*
*and the political prisoners . . . ?*
*It's always the people who are left in their anguish.*

*I want to reaffirm as a person of hope,*
*despite all these doubts, that I believe*
*a new ray of salvation will break through.*
*I want to hold out this hope to all those of good will*
*who are listening to me . . .*

*What we must preserve, above all,*
*is the liberation process of our people.*
*The people have already understood this process,*
*which has cost them so much blood,*
*and we dare not lose it.*
*We can overcome this present crisis*
*by bringing the process to its completion.*
*This is what we must try to do.*

*We must take our cue from the Gospel of the day and ask:*
*What is the star that must guide the people,*
*the government,*
*the different sectors of society?*

*How can we insure that this process of the people*
*in search of social justice not come to a halt,*
    *not fade out,*
    *but that it keep moving ahead?*

*Our people have common sense.*
*Our people know how to discern the difference*
    *between a false redemption and a true one.*
*They put their hope in those who offer them*
    *the true liberation they need . . .*
*May they seek their vocation.*
*May they reflect in the light of the Word.*
*Now is the time in which our people*
    *must carry out this task,*
    *creating new alternatives.*
*A simple adaptation of the old will not do.*

*There are new paths on which Christian inspiration*
*can carry our so deeply Christian people.*
*In this I am simply doing*
    *what Medellín recommends:*
*Conscientizing my people on the need*
    *to organize and participate,*
*so that our people may not be mere spectators*
*but rather authors of their own destiny.*
*I believe that those who truly wish to govern*
    *for the common good,*
*must count on the participation*
*of our noble Salvadoran people . . .*

Dennis Dunleavy

*Like Jerusalem, our country, too, is disturbed.*
*Government and people are disturbed about the future,*
*but as a church of hope, we, in imitation of the wise men,*
*know that somewhere*
    *He is here . . .*
*Make room for Jesus Christ!*
*Let the King of Peace come in!*
*Place before Him, with the humility of the wise men,*
    *a humble heart, seeking Him,*
*and we will find the solution for our country.*[205]

111

# The People's Project

Octavio Duran

On January 2, 1980, military and civilian members of the government met at the archdiocesan seminary to try and resolve the conflict, but to no avail. By the end of the day, the civilians had resigned from the government. Subsequently, a new government alliance, backed by the United States, was formed between the center-right Christian Democrats and the military high command.

On January 6, in his Epiphany homily, Romero called on the new government to place its hope in the common good of the people, not in the armed forces, and he publicly called on the Minister of Defense to resign. With his hope intact, Romero turned his attention to the people:

> *What we must preserve, above all, is the liberation process of our people. The people have already understood this process, which has cost them so much blood, and we dare not lose it. We can overcome this present crisis by bringing the process to its completion. This is what we must try to do.*[206]

In his homilies on January 13 and January 20, Romero analyzed the political options proposed to the country by the different sectors of society. The oligarchy and the extreme right represented structural injustice and violent repression, and offered no solution for the country: "In the name of our people and our church, I call on them to hear the voice of God and joyously share their power and wealth with all, instead of provoking a civil war that will bathe us in blood."[207]

The new government composed of Christian Democrats and the military promised reforms, but they provided only bloody repression. Each week, Romero read out a list of the murders and disappearances carried out by the government and the death squads closely aligned with it: "No government can ever become established that, along with its promises of change and social justice, is staining itself more each day, with the alarming reports that come to us from everywhere of repressive cruelty at the expense of the people themselves."[208]

Only the popular organizations provided hope for the people, with their vision of democratic government and social justice, but Romero was also critical of their resort to violence and failure to achieve unity. He called on all Salvadorans "to act in favor of justice with the means they have and not remain passive out of fear of the personal sacrifices and risks that every daring and truly effective action implies . . . and to use their critical sense, each one, and put it at the service of the common good."[209]

On January 22, the anniversary of the 1932 peasant uprising when thirty thousand peasants were massacred by the military, the popular organizations joined together in a show of unity and marched through the streets of San Salvador:

> Block after block was full of people. The demonstration was about eight kilometers long. I had a knot in my throat and in my heart. I'd gone not believing. I went to see if the popular organizations really had all the support they said they had. I didn't believe it. All of it was surprising to me. Such a huge crowd. Such order. Such awareness. Such happiness. It seemed to me more like a celebration. And it was . . . It was the first attempt to unite all of the groups on the left . . . I was practically crying, seeing it all. Two hundred thousand people!
>
> The march was so big, it was bound to end in bloodshed. From the very beginning, planes flew overhead spraying some kind of poison on the people . . . But everyone went ahead. Only a few turned back . . .
>
> When we got as far as the National Palace, the National Guardsmen, who were all holed up inside their lookout posts, started spraying—not poison, but bullets. I was in the Parque Libertad, and I could see everything. Then the panic started, the screams, the blood, the dead and the wounded hitting the pavement. And people looking for a place to hide . . . San Salvador seemed like a battlefield, smoldering after the exchange of fire.[210]

Despite the provocation, the people in the street showed restraint and, for the most part, did not respond with violence. But the days when the people could demonstrate peacefully were over. El Salvador was on the eve of civil war, and Romero did

Archbishop Romero in an audience with Pope John Paul II.
(Octavio Duran)

*"I want to use this occasion to reply to those who want to put me at odds with the Holy See. The archbishop of San Salvador is proud of being in communion with the Holy Father."*
—August 26, 1979

"If Christ had become incarnate now and were a thirty-year-old man today, he could be here in the cathedral and we wouldn't know him from the rest of you—a thirty-year-old man, a peasant from Nazareth, here in the cathedral like any peasant from our countryside."

—December 17, 1978

everything he could to prevent it. The following Sunday, Romero once again denounced the violence, as he told the people:

As pastor and as a Salvadoran citizen, I am deeply grieved that the organized sector of our people continues to be massacred merely for taking to the street in orderly fashion to petition for justice and liberty. I am sure that so much blood and so much pain caused to the families of so many victims will not be in vain.

It is blood and pain that will water and make fertile new and continually more numerous seeds—Salvadorans who will awaken to the responsibility they have to build a more just and human society—and that will bear fruit in the accomplishment of the daring, urgent, and radical structural reforms that our nation needs. This people's cry for liberation is a shout that rises up to God and that nothing and no one can now stop.[211]

The January 22 massacre forced Romero to postpone for a week a trip to Europe to receive an honorary degree from the Catholic University of Louvain, Belgium. On his way to Belgium, he stopped in Rome and received a surprise invitation from Pope John Paul II to a private audience:

He received me very warmly and told me that he understood perfectly how difficult the political situation in my country is; that he was concerned about the role of the Church; that we should be concerned not only with defending social justice and love of the poor, but also with what could result from a score-settling effort on the part of the popular left, which could also be bad for the Church.

I told him, "Holy Father, this is precisely the balance that I try to keep, because, on the one hand, I defend social justice, human rights, love of the poor. On the other, I am always greatly concerned for the role of the Church, and that by defending these human rights, we not become victims of ideologies that destroy feelings and human values."[212]

At the end of the audience, the pope embraced Romero and said he prayed every day for El Salvador. "I felt here God's confirmation and his strength for my poor ministry," Romero wrote in his diary.[213] The following day, Romero learned that Cardinal Lorscheider had come to Rome after his December visit to El Salvador and had given the pope a favorable report on him.

# Political Dimension of Faith

On February 2, 1980, Romero was at the Catholic University of Louvain in Belgium to receive an honorary degree and to speak on the topic "The Political Dimension of the Faith from the Perspective of the Option for the Poor." His words give some indication of what his fifth pastoral letter might have said, had he lived to write it.

He began his address by drawing attention to the world he was addressing, a world very different from the developed world of the North.

*Our Salvadoran world is no abstraction. It is not another example of what is understood by "world" in developed countries such as yours. It is a world made up mostly of men and women who are poor and oppressed. And we say of that world of the poor that it is the key to understanding the Christian faith, to understanding the activity of the Church and the political dimension of that faith and that ecclesial activity. It is the poor who tell us what the world is, and what the Church's service to the world should be.*[214]

Romero characterized the pastoral work of the Archdiocese of San Salvador as "a turning toward the world of the poor, to their real, concrete world." Even more, "experiencing these realities, and letting ourselves be affected by them, far from separating us from our faith, has sent us back to the world of the poor as to our true home. It has moved us, as a first, basic step, to take the world of the poor upon ourselves. It is there that we found the real faces of the poor."[215]

Precisely there, in the world of the poor, Romero encountered what Medellín had described as "that misery . . . that cries to the heavens," and Puebla as "the situation of inhuman poverty in which millions of Latin Americans live as the most devastating and humiliating kind of scourge."

*Peasants without land and without steady employment, without running water or electricity in their homes, without medical assistance when mothers give birth, and without schools for their children . . . Factory workers who have no labor*

*"I come from the smallest country in faraway Latin America. I come bringing in my heart, which is that of a Salvadoran Christian and pastor, greetings, gratitude, and the joy of sharing the experiences of life."*

—Louvain address, February 2, 1980

115

*"We have a better knowledge of what sin is. We know what offends God is the death for humans . . . Sin killed the Son of God, and sin is what goes on killing the children of God."*
—Louvain address

*rights, and who get fired from their jobs if they demand such rights, human beings who are at the mercy of cold economic calculations . . . Mothers and the wives of those who have disappeared, or who are political prisoners . . . Shantytown dwellers, whose wretchedness defies imagination, suffering the permanent mockery of the mansion nearby.*[216]

In this world "devoid of a human face," Romero saw "the sacrament of the suffering servant of Yahweh," and through this encounter with the poor, he discovered the central truth of the Gospel that calls us to set our feet firmly in the world of the poor in order to proclaim the good news with credibility:

*The church has to proclaim the good news to the poor. Those who, in this-worldly terms, have heard bad news, and who have lived even worse realities, are now listening through the church to the word of Jesus: "The kingdom of God is at hand; blessed are you who are poor, for the kingdom of God is yours." And hence they also have good news to proclaim to the rich: that they, too, become poor in order to share the benefits of the kingdom with the poor.*[217]

When the Gospel is proclaimed by a church which has incarnated its mission in the world of the poor, something astounding happens, what Romero described as "a coming together of the aspiration on our continent for liberation, and God's offer of love to the poor."

*It is something new among our people that today the poor see in the church a source of hope and a support for their noble struggle for liberation . . . It is support, sometimes critical support, for their just causes and demands . . . The hope that we preach to the poor is intended to give them back their dignity, to encourage them to take charge of their own future. In a word, the church has not only turned toward the poor, it has made of the poor the special beneficiaries of its mission.*[218]

Romero spoke of defending the poor as a necessary consequence of incarnating the church in the world of the poor and proclaiming the Gospel as good news to them.

*The church has not only incarnated itself in the world of the poor, giving them hope; it has also firmly committed itself to their defense. The majority of the poor in our country are oppressed and repressed daily by economic and political structures. The terrible words spoken by the prophets of Israel con-*

*tinue to be verified among us. Among us there are those who sell others for money, who sell a poor person for a pair of sandals; those who, in their mansions, pile up violence and plunder; those who crush the poor.*[219]

For Romero, the voices of the prophets are not just "voices from distant centuries . . . they are everyday realities" that point to the grief of the mothers of the disappeared, as well as to the cruel assassinations of those who struggle for justice and peace. In such a situation of violence and conflict,

Octavio Duran

*[t]he church has placed itself at the side of the poor and has undertaken their defense. The church cannot do otherwise, for it remembers that Jesus had pity on the multitude. But by defending the poor it has entered into serious conflict with the powerful who belong to the moneyed oligarchies and with the political and military authorities of the state. This defense of the poor in a world deep in conflict has occasioned something new in the recent history of our church: persecution.*[220]

The journey of incarnation in the world of the poor, then, which begins with a proclamation of good news to the poor, and progresses to a vigorous defense of their just demands and their lives, ends in persecution. In less than three years, six priests had been martyred, hundreds of people had been tortured and disappeared, and thousands more had been assassinated.

*Real persecution has been directed against the poor, the body of Christ in history today. They, like Jesus, are the crucified, the persecuted servant of Yahweh. They are the ones who make up in their own bodies that which is lacking in the passion of Christ. And for that reason when the church has organized and united itself around the hopes and anxieties of the poor it has incurred the same fate as that of Jesus and of the poor: persecution.*[221]

What Romero described as "the political dimension of the faith from the perspective of the option for the poor" was what he so faithfully put into practice in his own archdiocese.

Romero's episcopal motto: Sentir con la Iglesia—to feel deeply with the church. (Octavio Duran)

*The political dimension of the faith is nothing other than the demands made upon it by . . . the socio-political world in which it exists . . . This demand is a fundamental one for the faith, and [one] the church cannot ignore . . . I am talking about an authentic option for the poor, of becoming incarnate in their world, of proclaiming good news to them, of giving them hope, of encouraging them to engage in a liberating praxis, of defending their cause and of sharing their fate.[222]*

*There is put before the faith of the church, as it is put before the faith of every individual, the most fundamental choice: to be in favor of life or to be in favor of death. We see, with great clarity, that here neutrality is impossible. Either we serve the life of Salvadorans, or we are accomplices in their death. And here what is most fundamental about the faith is given expression in history: either we believe in a God of life, or we serve the idols of death.[223]*

Romero's address was well received in Belgium, but the situation in El Salvador continued to deteriorate. Upon his return, Romero was disturbed to learn that the United States was planning to send military aid to El Salvador, and he decided to write a letter to President Jimmy Carter. During his February 17 homily, he read the letter to the people gathered in the cathedral. Addressing President Carter, he said:

*Your government's contribution, instead of favoring greater justice and peace in El Salvador, will undoubtedly sharpen the injustice and the repression suffered by the organized people, whose struggle has often been for respect for their most basic human rights . . . If you truly want to defend human rights . . . guarantee that your government will not intervene . . . in determining the Salvadoran people's destiny.[224]*

# The Homily

During the three years that Romero was archbishop of San Salvador, "Sundays were truly holy days for the country's poor."

The Word of God, which sounded forth from the cathedral in San Salvador, touched the hearts of people throughout the country. Men, women, and children in every village, barrio, and cornfield of the nation tuned their transistor radios to listen to Monseñor's Sunday preaching . . . For Romero, it was a tremendous personal blessing and source of strength to know that his preaching was touching the lives of El Salvador's poor and forgotten masses.[225]

Octavio Duran

Many people who knew Romero remarked how he was transformed when he preached, and how carefully he prepared each homily.

Every week he met for several hours with a team of priests and lay people to reflect on the situation in the country, and afterwards he would put all of that reflection into his homilies. That was one of the keys to his sermons.

The other key was prayer. The meeting would end, he'd say good-bye to the group, and then he'd sit down to organize his ideas and prepare himself. I'm a witness, having seen him on more than one occasion in his room, on his knees, from 10:00 on Saturday night to 4:00 in the morning on Sunday, preparing his homily. He would sleep a little while and then be at the cathedral by 8:00.

He never wrote down his homilies. Never. It seemed like he did, but he didn't. The most he ever took to the cathedral was an outline, a letter-sized sheet of paper with two or three ideas written down. It makes me laugh when someone who never knew Monseñor Romero says that other people used to write his sermons. If anyone wrote them, it was the Holy Spirit![226]

Romero's last homilies are truly memorable achievements. The dramatic events of the day, the increasing violence in the country, the rapt attention of the thousands of faithful who listened to his words in the cathedral as well as throughout the country, and the impending certainty that he would be killed—all lent to his homilies an eloquence beyond measure.

All of El Salvador became a stage upon which Romero preached. When Romero read the letter to President Carter in his Sunday homily, he set in motion a series of events that sped the political drama toward its eventual conclusion and his own martyrdom. While the people applauded, the U.S. State Department and the Vatican were upset by his words to President Carter. The extreme right was not only upset, but angry. The following day, they bombed the church's radio station, YSAX.

Much of Romero's homily was taken up with sharing the address he had delivered the week before at the Catholic University of Louvain in Belgium. The readings for the day were from the Beatitudes, and drawing on Medellín, Romero spoke of the mystery of poverty as a denunciation of the inhuman conditions in which the poor live, a spirit of openness to do God's will, and a commitment to be in solidarity with the poor:

> This is the commitment of being a Christian: to follow Christ in his incarnation. If Christ, the God of majesty, became a lowly human and lived with the poor and even died on a cross like a slave, our Christian faith should also be lived in the same way. The Christian who does not want to live this commitment of solidarity with the poor is not worthy to be called a Christian.[227]

Then, as though with a premonition of the fate that awaited him, he alluded to the consequences of such a commitment of solidarity:

> Christ invites us not to fear persecution. Believe me, brothers and sisters, anyone committed to the poor must suffer the same fate as the poor. And in El Salvador we know the fate of the poor: to be taken away, to be tortured, to be jailed, to be found dead.[228]

Octavio Duran

Here we come to a key characteristic of Romero's preaching: his fidelity to living what he preached. He "taught with authority," that is, with credibility. No one doubted that what Romero preached was what he himself lived.

The key to his proclamation was the centrality of the poor, but especially the poor as regarded from the compassionate heart of God. Romero proclaimed the Gospel as one who knew the world of the poor, saw the world from their eyes, and shared their sufferings and hopes, and as one who knew the heart of God and God's compassion for the poor, as one who spoke on their behalf and defended their lives:

> *This is my greatest concern: to try to build with Christ a Church according to his heart . . . For that reason, I ask you to focus not only on the weekly events that the prophetic mission of the Church obliges me to illuminate, but also on the light that illuminates, on the attempt of this poor pastor to build a Church according to the heart of God.*[229]

Not only was Romero a prophet of God's Word to his people; such was his relation to the poor that he could say: "The people are my prophet."[230] He not only preached the Word of God to the people, he listened to the Word of God with the heart of the poor, with their hopes and joys, their sorrow and anguish, and walked with them as he helped them discern the way ahead.

> *The people of God, illuminated by their faith, look at their own aspirations, demands, and ideals. And with this faith, they know how to discern what God wants according to the signs of the times. Clearly not everything that people demand is the Word of God, but in the heart of the demands of our moment, there is much of God to be found, and here we have to discern.*[231]

For Romero, the proclamation of the Gospel each Sunday was a way in which he expressed the political dimension of our faith; an expression of his spirituality lived in dynamic relation to the poor and to the Gospel. To preach the Gospel meant to actualize the Word of God in the history of the people, giving it an eminently prophetic character.

It meant to discern the signs of God's presence in history and to announce them with hope, as well as to discern signs that were not of God and, accordingly, to denounce them.

*"I wish to affirm that my preaching is not political. It naturally touches on the political—and it touches the people's real lives—but it does so in order to illuminate those realities and to tell people what it is that God wants and what it is that he does not want."*

—January 21, 1979

*We not only read the Bible, we analyze it, we celebrate it, we incarnate it [in our reality], and we want to make it our life. This is the meaning of the homily: to incarnate the Word of God in our people. This is not politics. When we point out the political, social, and economic sins in the homily, this is the Word of God incarnate in our reality, a reality that often does not reflect the Reign of God but rather sin. We [proclaim the Gospel] to point out to people the paths of redemption.*[232]

*In the most sublime homily ever proclaimed, Christ closes the book and says: "Today these things have been fulfilled." This is the homily: the Word of God is not a reading of the past but a living Word, a Spirit that is being accomplished here and now. [What follows is] the effort to apply the eternal message of God to the concrete circumstances of the people.*[233]

Romero was the bridge between the Word of God and the cry of the poor. He went before God as a pastor with the cry of his people, and he went before his people as a prophet with the Word of God.

Courtesy of Equipo Maiz

# The Final Weeks

D uring the last week of February 1980, Archbishop Romero made his annual retreat with six priests from the vicariate of Chalatenango in Planes de Renderos, a retreat house located in the hills overlooking San Salvador. Romero's Jesuit confessor, Secundo Azcue, visited him at the retreat house. He later wrote:

> I dare to consider this last retreat of his as his prayer in the garden . . . Archbishop Romero foresaw his very probable and imminent death. He felt terror at it as Jesus did in the garden. But he did not leave his post and his duty, ready to drink the chalice that the Father might give him to drink.[234]

Romero had received warnings of imminent dangers he would face in the coming week, and he expressed his fear of death to his confessor, who encouraged him to give his life for God, whatever might be the end of his life: "My principal concern," Romero noted, "will be to become more identified with Jesus each day, accepting his gospel more radically."[235]

Romero then prayed the prayer of offering that St. Ignatius recommends to retreatants in his meditation on the reign of God, and added:

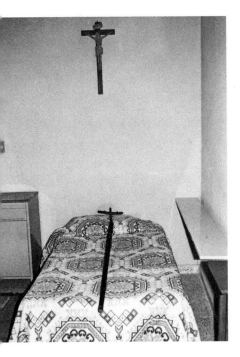

The archbishop's crosier rests on his bed. (James Brockman, S.J.)

*Thus do I express my consecration to the heart of Jesus, who was ever a source of inspiration and joy in my life. Thus also I place under his loving providence all my life and I accept with faith in him my death, however hard it be. I do not want to express an intention to him, such as that my death be for my country's peace or our church's flourishing. Christ's heart will know how to direct it to the purpose he wishes.*

*For me to be happy and confident, it is sufficient to know with assurance that in him is my life and my death, that in spite of my sins I have placed my trust in him and I will not be confounded, and others will continue with greater wisdom and holiness the works of the church and the nation.*[236]

Following the retreat, Romero preached again on the meaning of Lent amid the ongoing violence in the nation.

*This Lent, which we observe amidst blood and sorrow, ought to presage a transfiguration of our people, a resurrection of our nation . . . In poor lands, in homes where there is hunger, Lent should be observed in order to give to the sacrifice that is everyday life the meaning of the cross. But it should not be out of a mistaken sense of resignation. God does not want that. Rather, feeling in one's own flesh the consequences of sin and injustice, one is stimulated to work for social justice and a genuine love for the poor. Our Lent should awaken a sense of social justice.*[237]

In the weeks following his retreat, Romero continued to denounce the violence, and he called on the army in particular to end their occupation of entire rural areas.

*We do not overlook the sins of the left. But they are not in proportion to the amount of repressive violence . . . The 70 killings by the security forces and the so-called paramilitary forces had almost nothing to do with repelling these subversive attacks. They are part, rather, of a general program of annihilation of those of the left, who by themselves would not commit violence or further it were it not for the social injustice that they want to do away with.*[238]

On March 7, the government announced the long-awaited land reform and the nationalization of the banks. They were measures supported by the Christian Democrat–military junta, but fiercely opposed by the oligarchy and the extreme right. While Romero shared the goals of both reforms, he denounced the manner in which they were being carried out as "reforms bathed in blood."

Members of the center-right Christian Democratic Party were also being targeted for assassination. One of their members, Mario Zamora, had been killed the week before by right-wing death squads. Christian Democrats who still served in the government resigned on March 10 in protest. Napoleon Duarte, the party's head and an opportunist, offered to join the military officials and to create a new government.

Meanwhile, the repression continued. Security forces in San Salvador raided the parish of Zacamil, fired on persons occupying the church of El Rosario, and bombed the priests' cooperative, the weekly independent newspaper *El Independiente*, and the locale of the Mothers of the Disappeared.

Romero with his driver.
(Courtesy Maryknoll Archives)

In the rural areas, the repression was even worse. National Guard troops and paramilitary members of ORDEN invaded rural villages, burning houses and crops, and killing parents before the eyes of their children. Military operations in rural areas left dozens of people dead.

On March 16 Romero established two more centers near the San José de la Montaña seminary and the Domus Mariae retreat house to take in people displaced by the violence.

"They even broke the stones we use to grind our corn, those ingrates!" That's what the poor women from Cinquera said as they came in crying. They arrived with only the clothes they were wearing and their children in their arms. They had come asking for a place to stay in the seminary. They were fleeing the "agrarian reform."

Around that time, we already had two thousand campesino refugees in the patios and gardens of the arch-

*"Each country has its own promised land in the territory that geography has allotted it. We must always bear in mind and never forget this theological reality: the land is a sign of justice and reconciliation."*
—March 16, 1980

diocesan offices. Hundreds more were in other church buildings. There was such a continuous daily influx that there wasn't time to count them all. The only crime those refugees had committed was to be poor and to be part of an organized group . . .

There were three of us doctors attending to these people, working up to 10 hours a day. A hundred patients a day . . . It wasn't easy! Ninety-five percent of the refugees were women, children and old people. And half were children who were malnourished and full of parasites. We saw more gastrointestinal problems than anything else. And along with that, the neuroses—trauma left like fingerprints of the atrocities of military operations in the countryside.[239]

Also on March 16 Romero preached one of his longest sermons, one hour and three-quarters, appealing for reconciliation. *Nothing is so important to the church as human life, as the human person, above all, the person of the poor and the oppressed, who, besides being human beings, are also divine beings, since Jesus said that whatever is done to them he takes as done to him. That bloodshed, those deaths, are beyond all politics. They touch the very heart of God.*[240]

The following day, a general strike called by the popular organizations was met with more military repression.

"Monseñor, you're going to get killed," some of us told him. "Fine, don't accept the protection the government is offering you. But at least be careful and take the same security measures like all of the leaders of the grassroots organizations are doing . . . Don't do anything at the same time every day. Vary your schedule. Say Masses at different times than the ones you usually say . . . Don't drive your car yourself . . ."[241]

People say . . . that there have been several occasions now when they've seen Monseñor Romero driving his little car alone down the streets of San Salvador . . ."Why, Monseñor?" they ask him. "I prefer it this way. When what I'm expecting to happen, happens, I want to be alone, so it's only me they get. I don't want anyone else to suffer."[242]

# Easter Is a Shout of Victory

Octavio Duran

B y March 1980, the death threats to Romero's life had become more frequent. The hour was fast approaching when he would be martyred by an assassin's bullet on March 24 as he consecrated the bread and wine on the altar. A few days before Romero was assassinated, he offered these words of faith and affirmation:

> *My life has been threatened many times. I have to confess that as a Christian, I don't believe in death without resurrection. If they kill me, I will rise again in the Salvadoran people.*[243]

On March 23, 1980, the fifth Sunday of Lent, Oscar Romero preached his last Sunday homily. Many remember this homily for his courageous call to the military to "stop the repression!" What precedes that call, however, is a beautiful homily that is vintage Romero and a wonderful window to the spirituality of a man who embodied the very paschal joy that he proclaimed so boldly.

> *Easter is a shout of victory! No one can extinguish that life that Christ resurrected. Not even death and hatred against Him and against His Church will be able to overcome it. He is the victor! Just as He will flourish in an Easter of unending resurrection, so it is necessary also to accompany Him in Lent, in a Holy Week that is cross, sacrifice, martyrdom . . . Happy are those who do not become offended by His cross!*
>
> *Lent, then, is a call to celebrate our redemption in that difficult complex of cross and victory. Our people are very qualified . . . to preach to us of the cross; but all who have Christian faith and hope know that behind this Calvary of El Salvador is our Easter, our resurrection, and that is the hope of the Christian people.*[244]

Cross and resurrection, death and life: these are the cardinal points of Romero's spirituality. And they are linked, not sequentially, as though the way of the cross ultimately leads to resurrection. Already, in the midst of the cruelest passion that his people were living, the spirit of resurrection penetrates the darkness and offers light and hope to the poor.

*Today, as diverse historical projects emerge for our people, we can be sure that victory will be had by the one that best reflects the plan of God. And this is the mission of the Church . . . to see how the plan of God is being reflected or disdained in our midst . . .*

*That is why I ask the Lord during the week, as I gather the cry of the people, the aches of so much crime, and the ignominy of so much violence, that He give me the suitable word to console, to denounce, to call for repentance; and even though I may continue to be a voice crying in the desert, I know that the Church is making the effort to fulfill its mission.*[245]

*"'God's reign is already present on our earth in mystery. When the Lord comes, it will be brought to perfection.' That is the hope that inspires Christians. We know that every effort to better society, especially when injustice and sin are so ingrained, is an effort that God blesses, that God wants, that God demands of us."*

—March 24, 1980

In this last homily, Romero called attention to the dignity of the human person. In the midst of the life-and-death struggle of his people for liberation, in the midst of the terrible violence and repression of the military and death squads, Romero never lost sight of the human dignity of every person. Every person is a child of God, the Body of Christ, the Temple of the Holy Spirit.

*How easy it is to denounce structural injustice, institutionalized violence, social sin! And it is true, this sin is everywhere, but where are the roots of this social sin? In the heart of every human being. Present-day society is a sort of anonymous world in which no one is willing to admit guilt, and everyone is responsible. We are all sinners, and we have all contributed to this massive crime and violence in our country. Salvation begins with the human person, with human dignity, with saving every person from sin. And in Lent this is God's call: Be converted!*[246]

Respect for human dignity, however, requires working for the common good. God desires to save not only persons but also entire peoples. God's plan of salvation is to make the history of every people a history of salvation. And the mission of the church is to illuminate the way.

*Today El Salvador is living its own Exodus. Today we, too, are journeying to our liberation through the desert, where cadavers and anguished pain are devastating us, and where many suffer the temptation of those who were walking with Moses and who wanted to turn back . . . God desires to save the people making a new history . . . What is not repeated are the circumstances, the opportunities to which we are witnesses in El Salvador . . .*

*History will not perish; God sustains it. That is why I say that in the measure that the historical projects attempt to reflect the eternal project that is God's, in that measure they are reflecting the Reign of God, and this is the work of the Church. Because of this, the Church, the people of God in history, is not installed in any one social system, in any political organization, in any political party . . . She is the eternal pilgrim of history and is indicating at every historical moment what reflects the Reign of God and what does not. She is the servant of the Reign of God.*[247]

Finally, Romero speaks of the transcendent dimension of liberation, what he calls the true or "definitive liberation." Here, too, the logic of the cross and resurrection applies. It is not by avoiding the demands of historical liberation that one reaches a definitive liberation, as though by avoiding the suffering of the cross one attains resurrection. It is precisely by incarnating our lives in the historical struggles of our time—and especially those of the poor—that we discover God's plan and promise of salvation.

*The true solution has to fit into the definitive plan of God. Every solution we seek—a better land distribution, a better administration and distribution of wealth in El Salvador, a political organization structured around the common good of Salvadorans—these must be sought always within the context of definitive liberation . . . Without God, there can be no true concept of liberation. Temporary liberations, yes; but definitive, solid liberations—only people of faith can reach them . . .*

*Do you see how life recovers all of its meaning? And suffering then becomes a communion with Christ, the Christ that suffers, and death is a communion with the death that redeemed the world? Who can feel worthless before this treasure that one finds in Christ, that gives meaning to sickness, to pain, to oppression, to torture, to marginalization? No one is conquered, no one; even though they put you under the boot of oppression and of repression, whoever believes in Christ knows that she is a victor and that the definitive victory will be that of truth and justice!*[248]

These three themes—the dignity of the human person, the salvation of people in history, and the transcendent dimension of liberation—form the heart of Romero's spirituality, and they

Octavio Duran

may be found in almost every homily that he preached as archbishop of San Salvador. Here, too, we find the centrality of the poor, the Gospel proclaimed as Good News to the poor, the necessity to defend the lives of the poor from encroaching death, and the witness of the poor sealed in the blood of martyrdom.

Oscar Romero knew as well as anyone that to proclaim the Gospel in word and deed—announcing God's salvation and denouncing evil by name—is to invite enemies to your doorstep. Jesus, too, had enemies; the four Gospels are clear on that account. The remarkable thing, however, is that Romero, like Jesus, loved his enemies—he called them "brothers"—and that is why he called them to account. His love for his enemies, however, was rooted in his love for the poor and his love for the Gospel. That is why he spoke the truth and demanded justice.

*"I beseech you, I beg you, I command you in the name of God: 'Stop the repression!'"*

> *I would like to appeal in a special way to the men of the Army, and in particular to the troops of the National Guard, the police, and the garrisons. Brothers, you belong to our own people. You kill your own brother peasants; and in the face of an order to kill that is given by a man, the law of God should prevail that says: "Do not kill!" No soldier is obliged to obey an order counter to the law of God. No one has to comply with an immoral law. It is time now that you recover your conscience and obey its dictates rather than the command of sin.*
>
> *The Church, the defender of the rights of God, of the law of God, of the dignity of the human person, cannot remain silent before so much abomination. We want the government seriously to consider that reforms mean nothing when they come bathed in so much blood. Therefore, in the name of God, and in the name of this long-suffering people, whose laments rise to heaven every day more tumultuous, I beseech you, I beg you, I command you in the name of God: "Stop the repression!"*[249]

# Unless a Seed Die

Like his friend Rutilio Grande, Romero "died loving" his enemies; and like the figure of the Bedouin in the desert—whose image he evoked in the funeral Mass of Alfonso Navarro—Romero died pointing the way to forgiveness and life: "Not there, but here." In the end, Romero forgave his assassins. In an interview with journalists shortly before his death, he said:

> *You can tell people, if they succeed in killing me, that I forgive and bless those who do it. Hopefully, they will realize that they are wasting their time. A bishop will die, but the Church of God, which is the people, will never perish.*[250]

On March 24, 1980, Oscar Romero was assassinated while celebrating the anniversary Mass of a friend's death in the chapel of the Divine Providence Hospital,[251] the hospice for cancer patients in San Salvador, and his place of residency.

The chapel of the Divine Providence Hospital, where Romero was shot while celebrating Mass. (Octavio Duran)

> *Whoever offers their life out of love for Christ, and in service to others, will live like the seed that dies ... May this immolated body and this blood sacrificed for all nourish us so that we may offer our body and our blood as Christ did, and thus bring justice and peace to our people. Let us join together, then, in the faith and hope of this intimate moment of prayer.*[252]

With these words, Oscar Romero fell to the ground, mortally wounded in the heart by a single bullet from an assassin's gun that pierced his heart as he lifted up the cup of wine in the offertory of the Mass. In the days and weeks before his assassination, Romero had already begun to prepare himself for the eventuality of his martyrdom. In the last retreat he made, a few weeks before his death, he told his spiritual director:

> *My other fear is for my life. It is not easy to accept a violent death, which is very possible in these circumstances ... You have encouraged me, reminding me that my attitude should be to hand my life over to God regardless of the end to which that*

*life might come; that unknown circumstances can be faced with God's grace; that God assisted the martyrs, and that if it comes to this I shall feel God very close as I draw my last breath; but that more valiant than surrender in death is the surrender of one's whole life—a life lived for God.*[253]

The testimony of martyrdom is, in one sense, a tragic consequence of the conflict in El Salvador, and the cost paid by those who were faithful to the demands of the Gospel, taking sides with the poor, and offering their lives out of a fundamental option of love. Seen with the eyes of faith, the testimony of martyrs is one of the greatest treasures of the church. That is the way Romero saw it:

*I am glad, brothers and sisters, that our church is persecuted precisely for its preferential option for the poor and for trying to become incarnate in the interest of the poor and for saying to all the people, to rulers, to the rich and powerful: unless you become poor, unless you have a concern for the poverty of our people as though they were your own family, you will not be able to save society.*[254]

A view of the altar from the rear of the chapel. (James Brockman, S. J.)

Martyrdom, for Romero, was a sign of the church's fidelity to the Gospel, incarnating itself in the world of the poor, proclaiming the Good News, and taking up the defense of the poor even if it requires one's life. In this way, the Archdiocese of San Salvador fulfilled the mandate of the Second Vatican Council to make the joys and hopes, the anguish and the sorrow of the poor its own.[255]

Martyrdom brings credibility to the church precisely because it is a sign that the church is truly one with the poor, and with the sufferings and joys of its people. In Romero's words:

*It is the glory of our Church to have mixed its blood—the blood of its priests, catechists, and communities—with the massacres of the people, and ever to have borne the mark of persecution.*[256]

Octavio Duran

Each time he recalled the martyrdoms of Rutilio Grande, Alfonso Navarro, Octavio Ortíz, Rafael Palacios, Ernesto Barrera, and Alirio Napoleón Macías—the six priests killed in El Salvador during Romero's lifetime—Romero saw behind these more visible assassinations the vulnerability of the poor.

*If all this has happened to persons who are the most evident representatives of the church, you can guess what has hap-*

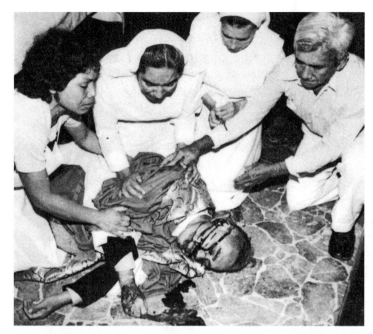

Friends rush to Archbishop
Romero's aid as he lies bleeding.
(Publicaciónes Pastorales del Arzobispado)

pened to ordinary Christians, to the campesinos, catechists, lay
ministers, and to the Christian base communities. There have
been threats, arrests, tortures, murders, numbering in the hundreds and thousands. As always, even in persecution, it has
been the poor among the Christians who have suffered most.[257]

And while martyrdom is a sign of the church's fidelity to the
Gospel, its deepest significance is that it reveals precisely what
being faithful to the Gospel means in a world in which the lives
of the poor are so much at risk.

*It is, then, an indisputable fact that, over the last three years,
our church has been persecuted. But it is important to note why
it has been persecuted. Not any and every priest has been persecuted, not any and every institution has been attacked. That
part of the church has been attacked and persecuted that put
itself on the side of the people and went to the people's defense.*[258]

The testimony of the martyrs, then, is intimately linked to
the poor, to proclaiming the Gospel as Good News to those who
have only known bad news, and to defending the life of those
whose lives are most at risk. Because the church in El Salvador
had placed the poor at the heart of its identity and its mission, it
was persecuted. But that is its glory. The same, of course, is true
of Oscar Romero. In the end, he became the Good News that he

*"The Church is glorified for
having mixed its blood with the
massacres of our people."*
—February 17, 1980

133

proclaimed to the poor.

> *As a pastor, I am obligated by divine commandment to give my life for those I love . . . even for those who would assassinate me . . . For that reason, I offer God my blood for the redemption and resurrection of El Salvador . . . Martyrdom is a grace that I don't believe I merit. But if God accepts the sacrifice of my life, may my blood be the seed of liberty and sign that this hope will soon become a reality. May my death, if it is accepted by God, be for the liberation of my people and a testimony of hope in the future.*[259]

In his life and in his death, Romero bore witness to the ancient wisdom of the church: "The blood of the martyrs is the seed of new Christians."[260] While he was archbishop, Romero reminded the world that the privileged place of the church is among those who suffer, wherever they may be. In the end, his death—like the death of so many martyrs who joined themselves to Christ in a generous offering of their lives—was redemptive. The Good News of the Gospel that Romero proclaimed continues to be an effective and encouraging presence in the lives of the poor today.

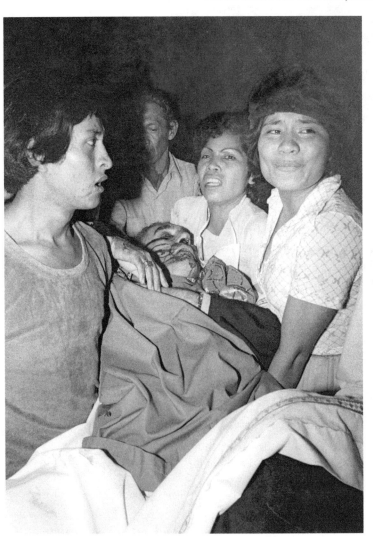

# The Funeral

Archbishop Romero was buried in a tomb in the cathedral of San Salvador, a few days after he was assassinated. His funeral Mass was attended by tens of thousands of poor who had come to pay their final respects to the pastor they loved. Tragically, the funeral itself became the occasion for further violence as the military and police fired shots into the crowds of people who had gathered in the plaza in front of the cathedral. Dozens of people were trampled to death in the desperate attempt to take refuge in the cathedral.

The significance of the violence at Romero's funeral Mass was not lost on Gustavo Gutiérrez, the "father" of liberation theology, who was there.

It was a tragic Sunday, as many will surely remember, when thirty or forty people were killed . . . Could Monseñor Romero, who wanted to give his life for his people, have been buried in a kind of oasis of peace? Many of us asked ourselves that question, almost discreetly, as we buried him two hours after being enclosed in the cathedral. Could he have been buried in isolation from the reality that his people lived daily? Unfortunately, it could not

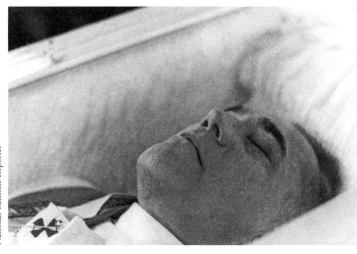

National Catholic Reporter

have been otherwise. Monseñor Romero's burial took place in the midst of the suffering and struggles of his people. [261]

The death of Archbishop Romero was an occasion for profound sorrow and—with time—of profound joy, the same sorrow and joy that Romero himself attributed to the commemorations of the martyrs over which he presided. In Gutiérrez's words:

[Romero's] death, in spite of the immense impact of sorrow that it brought us . . . was also a source of joy, because one could see in Monseñor Romero the integral witness of a Christian dedicated to announcing the Word, bearing witness to the Reign of God, and offering solidarity to those who suffered injustice. The integrity of his life is an example of something extraordinary.[262]

Gutiérrez further characterized the life and death of Romero as a watershed in the history of the Latin American church: "I think that we could say, without exaggeration, that the life and death of Monseñor Romero divides the recent history of the Latin American church into a before and after."[263] Like the martyrdoms that preceded Romero's, and those that came after, his death offers light and life to a church that has been, from its inception, a church of the martyrs and a church of the poor.

The martyrdom of Monseñor Romero allows us to see with greater clarity the witness of many other martyrdoms—of peasants, lay people, religious, and priests in Latin America: martyrdoms that many people scandalously still do not accept. The death of Monseñor Romero illuminates the sacrifice of their lives, and the lives of all those who unfortunately have followed. Romero's death is one of those deaths that bear witness to life in a profound way, even to a Church that, since its inception, has always lived and blossomed from the blood of the martyrs.[264]

The spirit of Oscar Romero found in the hearts of the poor bears witness to his prophetic insight: "If they kill me, I will be resurrected in the Salvadoran people."

Romero's coffin carried from the cathedral while crowds remain inside. (Equipo Maíz)

Oficina para la Causa de Canonización de Oscar Arnulfo Romero, Arzopisbado de San Salvador

136

Like the first generation of Christians, many of whom had known Jesus personally, the memory of Oscar Romero is alive in his people. And like the witness of the early Christian communities—who bore witness to the Spirit of the risen Christ in their midst—the poor in El Salvador continue to offer us the key to Romero's spirituality, a spirituality which, in its depths, bears witness to that same Spirit of the risen Christ.

> The secret of Monseñor Romero is simply that he resembled Jesus, and in our days, he continues to make Jesus present to us. He witnesses to the Witness . . . And for that reason, the eyes of many people are fixed on him, in the same way as the Letter to the Hebrews tells us to keep our eyes fixed on Jesus.[265]

Not only do the passion and death of Jesus illuminate the martyrdom of Archbishop Romero; Romero's death, in no small measure, has deepened the faith of the poor in Jesus Christ and led them back to the source of their faith and life. The spirit of Romero, as the spirit of the martyrs before him, brings us back to the heart of the paschal mystery. As another Salvadoran refugee testified:

> When they killed Monseñor Romero we were very sad, because we thought everything had ended. But later we saw that his spirit gave us strength to resist oppression. For that reason, we also believe more now in Jesus Christ.[266]

*"I have often received death threats. I must tell you that, as a Christian, I do not believe in death without resurrection. If they kill me I will rise again in the Salvadoran people."*
—March 1980

Some of those who died at the funeral, either from gunfire or crushed in the ensuing panic. (Octavio Duran)

137

# Life Has the Last Word

The spirit of Oscar Romero, then, through his memory and through his word, continues to be a prophetic presence in El Salvador—and throughout the world, offering the poor the comfort that they are not alone, and the promise that things can change.

His memory is a "subversive" one, in the sense that the Beatitudes are subversive: they remind us that the world is not meant to be as it is currently constituted, where the poor are excluded, the hungry forgotten, those who grieve hidden from view, and the victims blamed for their own persecution. Rather, the poor are blessed because theirs is the Reign of God. Life, not death, will have the last word.

In El Salvador—and increasingly so throughout Latin America—a crucified people continues to announce resurrection. At moments, there seem to be more shadows than light, more poverty and violence than hope for transformation, more death than life, more cross than resurrection. Testimony to that fact are these words of Jon Sobrino:

> In El Salvador, as well as in the entire Third World . . . an alarming situation still exists: inhumane poverty, cruel

The faithful gather at Romero's temporary tomb in the cathedral.
(Paul Newpower)

138

injustice, conflict and war, repression and the violation of human rights, disillusionment with the failures of the people, and all the suffering and darkness that this brings to the majority of the people who are poor. We all know this, but unless we are willing to deepen our awareness of it we will not be able to understand the importance of Monseñor Romero and his presence among us today.[267]

These words accurately describe the situation of the majority of the world's poor today. The fact that these words were spoken in 1990, on the occasion of the tenth anniversary of Romero's martyrdom, only underscores how grave is the situation for the poor in the Third World—what we now call the global South.

In 1995, on the fifteenth anniversary of Romero's death, Gustavo Gutiérrez recalled the deeper truth of Romero's martyrdom as he preached in the chapel of the Jesuit martyrs in San Salvador.

We come to this Eucharist to give thanks for Monseñor Romero, and for so many who have already been resurrected with Jesus, and who will continue to be resurrected . . . The martyrs remind us of Jesus' resurrection; they recall for us the center of our faith and of our hope. We must always remember—in communion with martyrs—that death does not put an end to our hopes and joys; life is the heart of the Christian message.[268]

Oscar Romero is important, not only because his prophetic word continues to illuminate "the signs of the times" and to judge the current social reality from the perspective of God's plan of salvation; his witness is essential today for the sake of our Christian faith.

If it were not for the testimony of the martyrs—if it were not for the witness of Oscar Romero—and the power of Jesus' resurrection to which the martyrs bear witness, so much suffering and death among the poor in El Salvador would have been in vain.

But the spirit of Oscar Romero—made present in the communal act of remembrance—has marked the poor forever, binding their passion and death to the passion and death of

139

Jesus Christ, and raising them to new life.

For that reason, the memory and spirit of Romero, like the memory and spirit of the martyrs, strengthens our faith in Jesus Christ, and in the power of the Gospel to bring Good News to the poor. This is the heart of the message that Gutiérrez proclaimed in his homily to the people of El Salvador:

> Today we celebrate a Eucharist, we recall a death, but we also know that for Christians—and Monseñor Romero and so many others have told us this with great clarity—death is not the last word of human existence; life has the last word . . . They can silence our voices—and here I am thinking of Romero's own words—but "they cannot silence the voice of hope and joy that we feel," this paschal joy that has overcome death.[269]

The force of the resurrection continues to be present in El Salvador, indeed, throughout the world, even in the midst of the crucifixion of the poor.

Because Oscar Romero was faithful to the poor, he joined his life to theirs and shared the same fate as the poor. Their passion became his passion, their crucifixion his cross. But because Romero was also faithful to the Gospel, he joined the passion of the poor to Christ's passion, and thus to Christ's resurrection. Just as God vindicated Jesus and raised him from the dead, so God has vindicated the martyrs—and Oscar Romero with them—and joined their resurrection to the resurrection of Christ.

The challenge today is continually to bring the poor, the Gospel, history, and the martyrs into the heart of the church and its pastoral mission:

> Monseñor Romero and the martyrs put forward the fundamental question for the Church: to be a people of God, an ecclesial body, followers of the mission of Jesus, and leaven in the country—all of this from the perspective of the poor, for the poor, and with the poor at the center . . . The martyrs were very clear about this: the poor, as poor, are the privileged ones of God, and should be at the heart of the Church, its doctrine, its hope, its mission, its celebration.[270]

Ignacio Ellacuría summarized the foundation of Romero's spirituality as follows:

> Monseñor Romero based his hope on two pillars: a historic pillar, that was his knowledge of his people for whom he attributed an unquenchable capacity to find solutions to their most grave difficulties; and a transcendent pillar, that was his belief that ultimately God is a God of life and not death, that the last word of reality is good and not evil. This hope not only enabled him to overcome any temptation of discouragement, it encouraged him to continue working, aware that his effort would not be in vain, regardless of how brief the time.[271]

*"If they kill me, you can say that I forgive and bless those who do it. Hopefully they will be convinced it is a waste of time. A bishop will die, but the Church of God, which is the people, will never perish."*
—March 1980

Speaking at the twenty-fifth anniversary celebration of Romero in 2005, Jon Sobrino described the legacy that Rutilio Grande, Archbishop Romero, Ignacio Ellacuría, and all of the Salvadoran martyrs had left behind as a torch to be passed on to present and future generations.

> In recent years the Salvadoran Church has passed through moments of Christian splendor. It has taken up the founding tradition of following Jesus and historicized that following into a stream. We can say that the stream was shaped this way: "When Rutilio Grande was murdered, Archbishop Romero began; when Archbishop Romero was murdered, Father Ellacuría began . . ."
>
> Each of them . . . and many other men and women . . . in his or her way, picked up the torch that the other had left. It was difficult and costly, but also joyful. They made something real out of the faith, Christianity, and the Church. That is what they have left to us.[272]

# An Enduring Legacy

I n the years since his martyrdom, the spirit and witness of Oscar Romero has spread throughout the world. In the words of Jon Sobrino, Romero has become "the most universal Christian at the end of the twentieth century."

Monseñor Romero inspires indigenous people and peasants, African Americans and oppressed, but also intellectuals, university professors, professionals, bishops, and humble catechists. Despite the passing of years, the commemoration of Romero's life has not diminished. In times of war and in times of peace, countless human beings continue to celebrate him. In Romero, that which is Christian and that which is human is very present.[273]

*"Sooner or later the voice of justice will triumph for our people."* —February 15, 1980

This universal presence was amply confirmed at the twenty-fifth commemoration of Romero's martyrdom in 2005.[274] To share but one example, among those present at the celebration at the UCA in San Salvador was Bishop Kevin Dowling, a Redemptorist from South Africa, who gave testimony to Romero's influence in his life.

When I became a bishop in the apartheid regime in South Africa, it was Oscar Romero who inspired me to reflect on my calling as a spiritual leader in the midst of my oppressed people where I lived and ministered. He was my brother, my mentor, whose witness challenged me to take a prophetic stance (a very personal form of suffering) and to walk with the poor—even if this meant danger to my life. Because of him, I tried to see the face of Jesus in the face of my oppressed people.[275]

Bishop Dowling's humble demeanor reminded many of Oscar Romero. He spoke of the challenges people faced under the apartheid regime, and the many risks he himself undertook.

I experienced something (a very small part) of the loneliness and pain of my brother Oscar Romero. On the many occasions when I had to suffer danger and rejection, I felt his close presence and inspiration. In 1997, I was called by the Truth and Reconciliation Commission to testify about two incidents of injustice and oppression. I was so humbled as I sat next to women who had been brutally raped by the security police because they opposed the regime. Yes, I truly felt on that day that God had blessed me abundantly in being able to share in some small way the suffering of the poor and oppressed.

So often I remembered the pilgrimage which Oscar Romero shared with the poor and oppressed of El Salvador. I thank you, dear brother of mine, Monseñor Romero, for showing me the way to be faithful to God in the life and suffering of the poor and oppressed of my land.[276]

Bishop Dowling spoke of "the brutalities of oppression, violence, genocide, war crimes and other atrocities in the world"—including the genocide in Rwanda, the ethnic cleansing in the Balkans, and the mass slaughter in the Darfur region of Sudan and in the Congo—as well as "the economic systems that trap the poor of the world in a cycle of hopelessness as they are sacrificed on the altar of greed."

Why is all this happening?

Because the economic systems of the world, controlled by the rich and powerful, condemn the countries of Africa, and the rest of the poorest nations on earth, to this kind of subhuman existence . . . by imposing terrible debt burdens that exceed the amount poor countries can spend on health, education and social services; and totally unfair trading systems that make it impossible for poor countries to compete with the rich and developed world.[277]

And where ought the church stand in relation to all this?

Our Catholic Social Teaching, which Monseñor Romero lived out with such courage and faith, calls us to see the face of Jesus in every face, but more especially in the little

Archbishop Romero's final tomb in the cathedral. (Octavio Duran)

ones. It challenges us to prophetic action so that the common good, solidarity, and above all the primacy of the poor become a goal that is being realized, rather than an impossible dream . . .

What our world today needs more than ever is an ethic of justice. We have to struggle for justice without which there will be no true peace or security. We have to struggle for a justice that is infused with the spirit of compassion and solidarity, so that the poor feel the presence of the God who cries when the poor of our world cry. And until we cry each time the poor cry, we will not be filled with the anger and the passion that will drive us to struggle for justice—no matter what the cost.[278]

Bishop Dowling shared the story of a young mother and her child dying of AIDS, and the mother's dying words to him: " 'Father, there is no hope; Father I have no hope.' Tears ran down her face and mine as she looked at her dying baby."

As I looked into the eyes of that young mother, I asked myself again the many questions that I carry in my heart. I think of our Church . . . Is our word, is the message of the Church truly experienced by the poor as a word of hope, a word of liberation, a word which challenges the reality which the poor feel so deeply?

Where are the prophets of the Church today who analyze the oppressive systems of the modern world from the perspective of the Gospel and the poor, and fearlessly stand with the poor in the quest to transform a world that becomes more and more unjust, a world where the gap between rich and poor grows steadily greater?[279]

For Bishop Dowling, the witness of Oscar Romero provides a credible response to these questions about the church: "I truly believe that Romero's word, his challenge, is as relevant for me and for us today as it was in 1980 for the people and church of El Salvador . . . I rejoice in you as God's gift to me and my people of South Africa. You have shown that Jesus' desire can and must be fulfilled, Jesus who said: 'I have come so that they may have life, and life to the full' " (John 10:10).[280]

# Communion of Saints

In her book *Friends of God and Prophets*, Elizabeth Johnson attempts to retrieve the "sleeping symbol" of the communion of saints. She writes:

> The communion of saints is a Christian symbol that speaks of profound relationship. In traditional usage, it points to an ongoing connection between the living and the dead, implying that the dead have found new life thanks to the merciful power of God. It also posits a bond of companionship among living persons themselves who, though widely separated geographically, form one church community.[281]

This is the traditional way that Christians over the centuries have understood this symbol, praying with devotion to their patron saints to intercede for their needs and for their loved ones, feeling a bond with loved ones who had died and with Christians throughout the world. But in more recent times, as faith increasingly has been linked to justice, and sanctity to contemporary saints and martyrs, the deeper meaning of the symbol has been awakened.

Octavio Duran

> Together the living form with the dead one community of memory and hope, a holy people touched with the fire of the Spirit, summoned to go forth as companions bringing the face of divine compassion into everyday life and the great struggles of history, wrestling with evil, and delighting even now when fragments of justice, peace, and healing gain however small a foothold.[282]

This way of understanding the communion of saints—as a community of memory and hope linked to solidarity—provides us with a fruitful framework for remembering Archbishop Romero. Even in the midst of the cruelest passion of his people, Romero lived with a spirit of resurrection, penetrating the

Octavio Duran

darkness with the Word of God and offering light and hope to the poor by his Gospel witness.

For Christians, "the memory and hope of the Christian community of faith are grounded on the foundational narrative and witness of the life, death, and resurrection of Jesus the Christ."[283]

> At the heart of biblical and liturgical proclamation is the *memoria passionis, mortis, et resurrectionis Jesu Christi* [memory of the passion, death, and resurrection of Jesus Christ], a very definite memory of concrete suffering, injustice, violence, and death, and through this of God's victory over evil and death that grounds the promise of future freedom for the entire world. The effective power of this memory with its hope of a future, promised but unknown, sustains the communities' efforts to live faithfully and compassionately in the world even now. As with any critical memory, remembrance of the crucified and risen Jesus Christ is dangerous in a particular way . . .
>
> The memory of the passion summons up in a special way the concrete crosses of so many historical victims vanquished by injustice, persons defined by dominant voices as unimportant, while hope in the resurrection anticipates a liberating future precisely for them.[284]

Johann Baptist Metz offers us a theological framework for understanding memory, hope, and commitment in this way. Memory becomes a "subversive" memory, hope becomes a "liberating" future, and commitment is embodied in a narrative of resistance and a practice of solidarity with the poor.

One of the ways that powerful and dominating governments have stripped oppressed people of their identity is to suppress their memory, their stories, their cultural traditions, and their liberating practices.

> By contrast, personal and corporate identity is formed when suppressed memory is aroused. Witness the fact that every protest and rebellion is fed by the subversive power of remembered sufferings and freedoms. Thus, memory is a practice that serves to rescue threatened or lost identity . . .

By evoking the sufferings and victories of the past, it startles those who are bored or despondent into movement. By lifting up the unfulfilled promise of past suffering, it galvanizes an unquenchable hope that new possibilities coming out of the past can be realized now, at last. By bringing "something more" into view, it awakens protest and resistance. In these ways, it operates as a practical, critical, liberating force that helps to forge deep historical identity.[285]

Metz calls this kind of remembrance "eschatological memory," because the "surplus of meaning"—the unfulfilled dreams—borne by the act of remembrance points to a liberating future filled with promise and hope. "Another world is possible!" The victims and those in solidarity with them are joined in a common struggle that carries the burden of suffering and generates hope for transformation.

In situations of tremendous injustice, solidarity among the victims themselves is expressed in initiatives mutually taken to resist, to hope, and to celebrate even in the midst of suffering. For those not directly affected by the particular victimization, solidarity is expressed in conversion toward those who suffer, not just being affected emotionally by their pain but choosing to love by taking it as one's own, joining the struggle for life for all.[286]

Here, perhaps, we touch upon the significance of Romero's life and the witness of his martyrdom, not only for his people, but also for the entire world. He showed us what it means to be fully human, to be fully alive—to be in solidarity with the poor and with the victims—and in this way he showed us as well what it means to be a Christian and to work for transformation.

That we celebrate Romero's presence among us today is Good News: it renews our faith and gives us hope; it shows us how to love. It encourages us to be more generous, more forgiving, more passionate in our love for justice, and more compassionate in our love for the poor. It restores our faith in justice and hope for humanity. And it renews our faith and hope in God.

When we remember Oscar Romero, we remember the mar-

*"Saint Romero of the Americas,*
*Our shepherd and our martyr,*
*No one shall ever silence*
*Your last homily."*
—Dom Pedro Casaldáliga

*"With Archbishop Romero, God has visited El Salvador."*
—Ignacio Ellacuría, S.J., martyred November 16, 1989

Octavio Duran

tyrs of the Salvadoran church, and we remember the entire communion of saints and litany of martyrs of the church throughout history. But most especially, we remember the one to whom Romero pledged his life, the Crucified and Risen One, Jesus Christ—and we remember the poor whom God loves in a special way.

It is among the poor that we find the true "friends of God, and prophets," and among the poor that we find the "community of memory and hope, a holy people touched with the fire of the Spirit, summoned to go forth as companions bringing the face of divine compassion into everyday life and the great struggles of history." It is among the poor, too, that we find Oscar Romero.

Truly, as we remember the martyrdom of Oscar Romero, we are surrounded by a cloud of witnesses, a communion of saints and martyrs. There, standing in the midst of that cloud, we will find Oscar Romero, the friend of God and prophets, the prophet-martyr of El Salvador, in whom great suffering and great love are joined as one. So, with faithful Christians throughout the world, we cry out with joy: "Oscar Romero . . . *Presente!*"

# The Word Remains

I n the summer of 1998, Westminster Abbey decided to fill ten niches on the West Façade, empty since the fifteenth century, with statues of outstanding Christian martyrs from the twentieth century.[287] In the words of the principal organizer of the event, their hope was "to proclaim a message of which too few people are aware: the twentieth century has been a century of Christian martyrdom."[288]

One of those ten martyrs honored by the abbey was Oscar Romero, who stands next to the statue of Dietrich Bonhoeffer, the German Lutheran pastor who was hanged April 9, 1945, for his resistance to the Nazi regime, and near the statue of Dr. Martin Luther King, Jr., the great prophet-martyr of the African American civil rights movement.

In *The Cost of Moral Leadership*, Geffrey Kelly and F. Burton Nelson recount the event at Westminster Abbey to make some insightful observations about these three twentieth-century martyrs:

> In the face of the civil legislation that in its malicious intent had targeted Jewish citizens for persecution, Bonhoeffer said that, at the very least, the church had to question the policies of the state and protest against them. Secondly, the church had to aid the victims, and not limit that help to those of the Christian faith. Finally, the church was obliged to oppose the government—as Bonhoeffer put it, [to] "jam a spoke in the wheel" of state . . .
>
> It is interesting to note that two of the martyrs honored with Bonhoeffer at Westminster Abbey in the summer of 1998, Martin Luther King and Archbishop Oscar Romero, both led their people in the same three steps urged by Bonhoeffer. Action for justice, whether for the beleaguered peasants of El Salvador or for the disenfranchised blacks of the United States, was as much a part of their love for and obedience to Jesus Christ as it was for Bonhoeffer.[289]

*"Through Archbishop Romero the gospel was transformed into a word of good news to the poor, and a word of demand upon the mighty. Through this person of this world and for this time, the gospel once again became a gospel for our times, and showed that it is indeed a gospel for all times."* —Jon Sobrino, S.J.

These three martyrs shared remarkable qualities: a life-long struggle for justice and peace, a denunciation of militarism, and a critique of the ideology of national security that institutionalizes violence and war. As early as 1934, at an ecumenical conference in Fano, Denmark, Bonhoeffer preached on the idolatry of war and the challenge of peace.

> It is as though all the powers of the world had conspired together against peace . . . and behind it all a world which bristles with weapons as never before, a world which feverishly arms itself to guarantee peace through weaponry, a world whose idol has become the word security . . . Peace must be dared . . . It is the great venture![290]

In a similar vein, in 1967, Martin Luther King, Jr., gave his prophetic address at Riverside Church in New York, openly opposing the war in Vietnam.

> A true revolution of values will lay hand on the world order and say of war, "This way of settling differences is not just" . . . A nation that continues year after year to spend more money on military defense than on programs of social uplift is approaching spiritual death . . . Our only hope today lies in our ability to recapture the revolutionary spirit and go out into a sometimes hostile world declaring eternal hostility to poverty, racism, and militarism . . . We still have a choice today: nonviolent coexistence or violent co-annihilation.[291]

And in his fourth and final pastoral letter, "The Church's Mission amid the National Crisis," written in 1979, Archbishop Romero proclaimed:

> *Peoples are put into the hands of military elites, and are subjected to policies that oppress and repress all who oppose them, in the name of what is alleged to be total war . . . The judgment merited by the ideology of national security has, for Christians, been clearly expressed at Puebla: it is "not compatible with the Christian vision of the human being as responsible for carrying out a temporal project, and to its vision of the State as the administrator of the common good."*

Bloodstained vestments that Romero wore when he was shot. (Octavio Duran)

Archbishop Romero among the modern martyrs installed at Westminster Cathedral in London.

*The omnipotence of these national security regimes . . . turn national security into an idol, which, like the god Molech, demands the daily sacrifice of many victims in its name.*[292]

Each of these three martyrs stood in solidarity with the oppressed and stood against the powers of the State as it oppressed the Jews, the blacks, the Salvadoran poor. Each of them stood as faithful pastors of their people, leaders of their churches, and prophets of their time, willing to name the idols that oppressed the poor and pay the cost for standing with the poor against powerful economic interests and the violence of the State.

Oscar Romero, like Dietrich Bonhoeffer and Martin Luther King, Jr., was deeply rooted in the prophetic tradition of the Hebrew prophets, and a faithful witness to the Gospels and to Jesus Christ. Like them, he was a powerful preacher, and his words gave hope to his people that God is on the side of the poor and the oppressed, calling everyone to stand together in solidarity with them. The beloved community excludes no one, but demands conversion.

At this critical moment in history, remembering the story of Oscar Romero invites and challenges us, particularly in the United States, to ask: Where are we in this picture? Where is our church today, in the midst of a permanent war economy and an unending war on terror? What claim do these martyrs have on our lives in a world which "feverishly arms itself to guarantee peace," a world still characterized by "the giant

Octavio Duran

triplets of war, poverty, and racism," a world increasingly marked by "the idolatry of capitalism and national security?"

Sixty years ago, in the wake of the destruction of the Second World War, Albert Camus posed this challenge to Christians:

> The world expects of Christians that they will raise their voices so loudly and clearly and so formulate their protest that not even the simplest person can have the slightest doubt about what they are saying. Further, the world expects of Christians that they will eschew all fuzzy abstractions and plant themselves squarely in front of the bloody face of history. We stand in need of persons who have determined to speak directly and unmistakably and come what may, to stand by what they have said.[293]

Oscar Romero, perhaps more than any other Christian of the twentieth century, offered an authentic Christian response to Camus's challenge. That was why the Salvadoran poor applauded him so enthusiastically when he delivered his homilies each Sunday in the metropolitan cathedral. He did not disappoint their hopes, nor did he refrain from challenging them. He was a true prophet, a true servant of God.

In the end, his death—like the death of so many prophets, saints, and martyrs who joined themselves to Christ in a generous offering of their lives—was redemptive. The Good News of the Gospel that Romero proclaimed continues to inspire courage and commitment in all who have come to know and love him.

Romero's invitation to us is that we, too—as individuals and as a church—might be fertile ground upon which the Word of God may fall, bearing fruit in lives of fidelity to the Gospel and fidelity to justice, peace, and solidarity with the poor.

*The Word remains. This is the great consolation of one who preaches. My voice will disappear, but my word—which is Christ—will remain in the hearts of those who have wanted to receive it.*[294]

# Afterword

It helps, now and then, to step back and take a long view.
The kingdom is not only beyond our efforts,
it is even beyond our vision.
We accomplish in our lifetime only a tiny fraction
of the magnificent enterprise that is God's work.
Nothing we do is complete, which is a way of saying
that the kingdom always lies beyond us . . .

For some time now this prayer, popularly known as the "Romero prayer," has inspired thousands of people across the United States. It captures Romero's vision of the Reign of God, his deep trust in the providence of God, his awareness of the task to which we are called, and his humility, knowing that we are planting seeds that others will harvest.

No statement says all that could be said.
No prayer fully expresses our faith.
No confession brings perfection.
No pastoral visit brings wholeness.
No program accomplishes the church's mission.
No set of goals and objectives includes everything.
It may be incomplete,
but it is a beginning, a step along the way,
an opportunity for the Lord's grace to enter and do the rest . . .

A few years ago, James Brockman, SJ, Romero's biographer, commented that he could find no reference to this prayer in Archbishop Romero's writings. Close associates of Romero in the church in San Salvador were also at a loss to find any mention of this prayer in Romero's papers.

Some years later, light was shed on this mystery. A few short days before his death, Saginaw Bishop Ken Untener sent a note to Bishop Tom Gumbleton. The note revealed that the "Romero prayer" was in fact a prayer Bishop

Zoila Aurora Asturias and Eva del Carmen Asturias

Untener had written in 1979 for Cardinal Dearden to offer in a Mass for deceased priests in the Detroit diocese.[295]

What ought we to make of this prayer, now that we know it was not from Romero? Does that knowledge make a difference? Perhaps, we might receive it in the same spirit that we receive "The Prayer of Saint Francis," the prayer that begins "Make me an instrument of your peace . . ." We now know that this prayer is not from Saint Francis. It first appeared in France, prior to the First World War, on a prayer card with a devotional image of Saint Francis on it, intended for Third Order Franciscans.

Later the prayer appeared in English prayer books and was broadcast daily by the BBC prior to the Second World War. Finally, the prayer appeared in German prayer books in the postwar period—brought to Germany from England by German prisoners of war. Though Saint Francis was not the author, the prayer does capture the Franciscan spirit. [296]

Perhaps the Romero prayer, like the Saint Francis prayer, may be shared by people across borders as a prayer for peace, a prayer to emulate in our lives the deep commitment that Romero had to the liberation of the poor, to God's justice, and to Christ's peace.

> We may never see the end results, but that is the
>    difference
> between the master builder and the worker.
> We are workers, not master builders; ministers, not
>    messiahs.
> We are prophets of a future not our own.
> This is what we are about.
> We plant the seeds that one day will grow.
> We water seeds already planted,
> knowing that they hold future promise.
> We lay foundations that will need further development.
> We provide yeast that produces far beyond our
>    capabilities.
> We cannot do everything, and there is a sense of
>    liberation
> in realizing that. This enables us to do something,
> and to do it very well. Amen.[297]

# Postscript

## Bearing Witness and Bearing Fruit:
## The Legacy of Blessed Oscar Romero

On February 3, 2015, Pope Francis officially announced the beatification of Archbishop Oscar Romero of El Salvador as a martyr of the Church. His beatification ceremony took place three months later on May 23, in San Salvador. Church bells rang to mark the occasion as people watched and listened throughout the world. Thirty-five years had passed since Romero was killed at the altar while celebrating Mass, his death planned and financed by the Salvadoran military and the death squads.

Above: Crowd gathered in San Salvador on May 23, 2015, for the outdoor beatification ceremony for Oscar Romero. (Robert Ellsberg)

Left: At the moment when Romero's beatification was proclaimed this rainbow-colored solar nimbus appeared in the sky and remained for some time.
(Robert Ellsberg)

The commission of cardinals and the commission of theologians in Rome were unanimous: "His death was not only politically motivated, but due also to 'hatred of the faith' that, combined with charity, would not stay silent when faced with the injustice that implacably and cruelly afflicted the poor and their defenders."

Thirty-five years after Romero's martyrdom, and in the midst of a joyful celebration of his beatification as a martyr, many forget how brutal was the violence that condemned the poor and those who defended them to a cruel fate. For Romero suffered a prophet's fate, denouncing grave injustices and cruel violence, and announcing the Gospel promise of greater justice and the life for the poor. For that he was bitterly attacked by those whose misuse of wealth and power he condemned, both in society and in the church. Like the prophets of old, Archbishop Romero was "a sign of contradiction."

## A Martyr for Justice and for the Option for the Poor

*"A church that doesn't provoke any crises, a gospel that does not unsettle, a word of God that does not get under anyone's skin, a word of God that does not touch the real sin of society in which it is being proclaimed—what gospel is that?"*

—Archbishop Romero, April 16, 1978

The martyr's relics (a bloodstained shirt) installed in the Cathedral of San Salvador. (Robert Ellsberg)

These prophetic words exemplify "the option for the poor" that marked much of the church in Latin America for decades after the historic meeting of Latin American bishops in Medellín, Colombia, in 1968. One of those bishops, Samuel Ruíz from Mexico, presided at the thirtieth anniversary Mass of Romero's martyrdom in 2010. His words are important, because they remind us that Romero was above all "a martyr for justice and for the option for the poor." Bishop Ruíz recalled a declaration that he and a group of Latin American bishops signed at Romero's funeral in 1980. In part it declared:

We admire and give thanks for three things. First, Archbishop Romero announced the faith and was master of the truth; second, he was a zealous defender of justice, and third, he was friend, bother and defender of the poor and oppressed, of peasants and workers, of those who live in the marginal communities. He was an exemplary bishop because he was a bishop of the poor in a continent that is cruelly marked by the poverty of the great majority; he made his place among the poor, defended their cause, and suffered the same fate as them: persecution and martyrdom.

His death was not isolated, but formed part of the witness of a Church which, since Medellín and Puebla, opted from a Gospel stance for the poor and oppressed. For that reason we understand better the death by hunger and sickness, the permanent reality of our peoples; as well as the numerous martyrdoms and crosses which have been borne by our continent in these years. These deaths are like that of Jesus: the fruit of injustice and the seed of resurrection.

## A Poor Church of the Poor in a World Filled with Crosses

*There is put before the faith of the church . . . the most fundamental choice: to be in favor of life or to be in favor of death. We see, with great clarity, that here neutrality is impossible. Either we serve the life of Salvadorans, or we are accomplices in their death. And here what is most fundamental about the faith is given expression in history: either we believe in a God of life, or we serve the idols of death"*

—Archbishop Romero, February 2, 1980

These words, spoken six weeks before Romero's martyrdom, remind us, as Pope Francis does today, of the promise and challenge of the Gospel. What do Pope Francis and Archbishop Romero have in common? For one, they shared the experience of Latin America, marked by grave inequalities and systemic injustice, military dictatorships and revolutionary movements, but also by solidarity, courageous social movements and hope. On the day of Romero's beatification, Pope Francis sent a message of "great joy," marking the event on the eve of the feast of Pentecost, the birth of the church: "Archbishop Romero, who built peace with the strength of love, gave witness to the faith with his life, given to the extreme."

In the midst of extremely difficult times, Pope Francis and Romero found real joy in the people, and hope! Romero commented often on the joy of his people and added: "I have to listen to the Spirit who speaks to me through his people. . . . The people are my prophet. . . . With this people it is not difficult to be a good shepherd." In a similar fashion, Pope Francis, in his Apostolic Exhortation, The Joy of the Gospel (EG 7), says: "I can say that the most beautiful and natural expressions of joy which I have seen in my life were in poor people who had little to hold on to."

The option for the poor was "the heart of Oscar Romero's spirituality and pastoral action." This is most evident in his Sunday homilies, where his voice became the voice of the voiceless, proclaiming the suffering and hope of his people. The same can be said of Pope Francis: "This is why I want a poor Church for the poor. We have to state, without mincing words, that there is an inseparable bond between our faith and the poor." Such an option has consequences, but that is what the Gospel calls us to. For Romero, "If the Church is faithful to her mission of denouncing the sin that brings misery to many, and if she proclaims her hope for a more just, humane world, then she is persecuted and calumniated, she is branded as subversive and communist." This is precisely the vision Pope Francis has for the Church:

> The thing the Church needs most today is the ability to heal wounds and to warm the hearts of the faithful; it needs nearness, proximity. I see the Church as a field hospital after the battle . . . to heal wounds. . . . I prefer a Church that is bruised, hurting and dirty because it has been out on the streets, rather than a Church which is unhealthy from being confined and from clinging to its own security.

## A Gospel of Life with the Heart of the Beatitudes

> *"Nothing is as important to the church as human life, as the human person, above all, the person of the poor and the oppressed, who, besides being human beings, are also divine beings, since Jesus said that whatever is done to them he takes as done to him. That bloodshed, those deaths, are beyond all politics. They touch the very heart of God."*
> —Archbishop Romero, March 16, 1980

To truly honor the memory of Oscar Romero, we must remember him as a courageous defender of human rights, a voice of the voiceless, who spoke truth to power in a conflictive moment in history. Accordiing to Jon Sobrino:

> Romero spoke out against the suffering of the people and pointed out those who were responsible. He exhorted the rich to share what they had with the poor in society. He roundly condemned the violence . . . and encouraged people to turn to social justice to avoid further bloodbaths. In the name of God, he demanded that the orders and commands of the military and police to kill innocent people be disobeyed.

Reflecting on the significance of the beatification, Sobrino links the true meaning of "blessed" in "Blessed Oscar Romero" to the Beatitudes in the Gospels: "Blessed are the poor . . . those who mourn . . . the meek . . . those who hunger and thirst for righteousness. . . . Blessed are the merciful . . . the pure in heart . . . the peacemakers . . . those who are persecuted for righteousness sake" (Mt 5:1-10). Those who, like Archbishop Romero, bear witness to and incarnate in their lives the spirit of the Beatitudes are blessed. They are, as he was, "salt of the earth" and "light of the world," those who "work for peace" and, in the final resort, those who "lay down their lives out of love for their friends." For Sobrino, Romero was somebody who embodied the spirit and practice of the Beatitudes, surrounded as he was by "a cloud of witnesses," those victims and martyrs whose names are among the 75,000 engraved on the memorial wall in San Salvador.

## Holy Ground and the Communion of Saints

*Together the living form with the dead one community of memory and hope, a holy people touched with the fire of the Spirit, summoned to go forth as companions bringing the face of divine compassion into everyday life and the great struggles of history, wrestling with evil, and delighting even now when fragments of justice, peace, and healing gain however small a foothold.*
—Elizabeth A. Johnson, CSJ, *Friends of God and Prophets*

This way of understanding the communion of saints—as a community of memory and hope linked to solidarity—provides us with a fruitful framework for remembering the martyrs, like Blessed Oscar Romero, and the victims, many of whom remain nameless and form part of what Ignacio Eliacuría called "the crucified people." They remind us of the first Christian martyr, Jesus of Nazareth. Even in the midst of the cruelest passion of their people, the saints and the martyrs live with a spirit of resurrection, penetrating the darkness and offering light and hope to us, the living, through their Gospel witness.

Thirty-five years after Romero's assassination, and twenty-five years after the conclusion of a brutal civil war, the root causes of the conflict continue to manifest themselves in the same divisions that Romero denounced during his brief three years as archbishop: "structural injustice," "institutionalized violence," and "social sin." No official apology has ever been made by a U.S. president for our complicity in the violence that produced 75,000 victims and displaced more than two million people from their homes. Such a solemn gesture, however, was made by ordinary citizens, some of whom had crossed the line at the School of Americas in Ft. Benning,

A campesino at the beatification ceremony shows his devotion.
(Robert Ellsberg)

Georgia and served time in prison to protest the training of Salvadoran soldiers responsible for so many murders, including that of Archbishop Romero, the six Jesuits, and the four North American churchwomen. Before the historic memorial wall in San Salvador that bears the names of the 75,000 victims, including Archbishop Romero, they read the following apology:

Today, we stand on Holy Ground, before this historic memorial to the victims and martyrs of the war, to humbly ask pardon for the complicity of our nation in bringing so much sorrow, so much destruction, and so much death to your people. . . . Thank you for your courage and dignity and humanity. Thank you for receiving our words asking pardon. We are sincere in saying that our lives have been forever changed and enriched because of your lives. You have shown us, and show the world, what it means to give your lives out of love for others, and to struggle unceasingly but with joy for another world founded on justice and solidarity.

Perhaps no better tribute to the legacy of Blessed Oscar Romero can be made by us than by making these words our own, and by accepting the invitation that Oscar Romero, together with the poor and the victims, offer us, expressed so well in these words of Dean Brackley, S.J., who made of his own life a faithful witness to the Gospel and a testimony of love for the poor:

It seems that the victims offer us the privileged place (although not the only place) to encounter the truth which sets us free. The poor usher us into the heart of reality. They bring us up against the world and ourselves all at once. . . . This outcast outside us calls forth the outcast within us. This is why people avoid the poor. But meeting them can heal us. We will only heal our inner divisions if we are also working to heal our social divisions. The victims of history—the destitute, abused women, oppressed minorities, all those the Bible calls "the poor"—not only put us in touch with the world and with ourselves, but also with the mercy of God. . . . They are a kind of door that opens before that Mystery and through which God passes to get at us. Clearly we need them more than they need us.

# NOTES

1 See Jon Sobrino, "Archbishop Romero: Some Personal Recollections," in *Witnesses to the Kingdom: The Martyrs of El Salvador and the Crucified Peoples* (Maryknoll, NY: Orbis Books, 2003), 11–53, and Jon Sobrino, *Archbishop Romero: Memories and Reflections* (Maryknoll, NY: Orbis Books, 1990).

2 See Monseñor Ricardo Urioste, "Archbishop Romero: A Saint for the 21st Century," May 2007. Talk given in London.

3 James Brockman, *Romero: A Life* (Maryknoll, NY: Orbis Books, 1989).

4 María López Vigil, *Oscar Romero: Memories in Mosaic,* trans. Kathy Ogle (Washington, DC: EPICA, 2000).

5 November 16, 2008, was the nineteenth anniversary of the assassination of the six Jesuits, their housekeeper, and her daughter. On that occasion, Pax Christi USA invited Jon Sobrino, SJ, to come to the vigil to close the School of the Americas at Ft. Benning, Georgia, and to receive an award for his most recent book, *No Salvation Outside the Poor: Prophetic-Utopian Essays* (Maryknoll, NY: Orbis Books, 2008).

6 Martin Maier, *Monseñor Romero: Maestro de espiritualidad* (San Salvador: UCA Editores, 2005), 21–22. The two paragraphs that follow are a paraphrase of Maier's inspirational biography. Ignacio Ellacuría, SJ, made similar comparisons.

7 *Carta a las Iglesias* (San Salvador: UCA Editores, 1981–), nos. 128 and 89. Author's translation unless otherwise noted.

8 Oscar Romero, "The Political Dimension of the Faith from the Perspective of the Option for the Poor," in Oscar Romero, *Voice of the Voiceless: The Four Pastoral Letters and Other Statements* (Maryknoll, NY; Orbis Books, 1985), 187. "Early Christians used to say *Gloria Dei, vivens homo* ('the glory of God is the living person'). We could make this more concrete by saying *Gloria Dei, vivens pauper* ('the glory of God is the living poor person')."

9 The Spanish word *campesino,* for "peasant," has become a familiar word in our English vocabulary, in part because of the many human rights reports from the 1980s that reported on the deaths and persecution of these rural farmworkers.

10 I was accompanied in this moment by Jim Harney, to whom this book is dedicated. Jim died December 26, 2008, after a recurrence of cancer. He chose to live his last months on a walk in solidarity with the undocumented. For an inspiring obituary, see Laura Foner and David Weinstein, "Jim Harney, 1940–2008," *The Nation,* February 6, 2009.

11 Elizabeth Johnson, *Friends of God and Prophets: A Feminist Theological Reading of the Communion of Saints* (New York: Continuum, 1998), 23.

12 Interview with *El Diario de Caracas,* March 19, 1980, in *La voz de los sin voz* (San Salvador: UCA Editores), 438–39. Author's translation.

13 Johnson, *Friends of God and Prophets.* I am indebted to this book for the idea of placing Romero's witness in the context of the communion of saints.

14 Jon Sobrino, SJ, cited on the back cover of *Oscar Romero: Reflections on His Life and Writings,* ed. Marie Dennis, Renny Golden, and Scott Wright (Maryknoll, NY: Orbis Books, 2000).

15 Johnson, *Friends of God and Prophets,* 23.

16 Gustavo Gutiérrez, in *Carta a las Iglesias,* no. 206.

17 For an excellent overview of El Salvador's history, see Robert Armstrong and Janet Shenk, *El Salvador: The Face of Revolution* (Boston: South End Press, 1982).

18 Between 1980 and 1992 the United States sent over $6 billion to the government of El Salvador, most of which was spent on direct military aid or economic support funds to bolster the war economy.

19 From *Madness to Hope: The Twelve-Year War in El Salvador,* Report of the Commission on the Truth for El Salvador, United Nations Office of Public Information.

[20] *The Washington Post,* March 17, 1993. "The chairman of a House subcommittee charged yesterday that the Reagan administration lied to Congress for years about the Salvadoran armed forces' complicity in murder, and he said that 'every word uttered by every Reagan administration official' about the observance of human rights in El Salvador should be reviewed for perjury. 'This Congress ten years ago established a process whereby President Reagan would certify that improvements were being made in human rights in order to continue military aid to El Salvador. It is now abundantly clear that Ronald Reagan made those certifications in defiance of the truth.'"

[21] *The New York Times,* March 25, 1993. "Declaring human rights central to United States policy, Secretary of State Warren Christopher appointed a panel today to investigate charges that State Department officials misled Congress about atrocities by the military in El Salvador throughout the 1980s."

[22] "Report of the Secretary of State's Panel on El Salvador," United States Department of State, July 1993.

[23] See Leslie Gill, *The School of the Americas: Military Training and Political Violence in the Americas* (Durham, NC: Duke University Press, 2004). "Salvadoran SOA graduate Major Roberto D'Aubuisson organized death squads and ordered the execution of Archbishop Oscar Romero" (84); "SOA graduate [General Jose Guillermo] Garcia failed to investigate the 1980 deaths of four U.S. churchwomen . . . and [General Carlos Eugenio] Vides Casanova, who headed the national guard at the time, allegedly ordered the murder of the nuns. Neither man was ever held accountable for these crimes, and Vides Casanova was invited to the School of the Americas as a guest speaker in 1983" (12); "Twenty-one of the soldiers who planned, executed, and covered up the massacre [of six Jesuit priests, their housekeeper, and her daughter] had attended the School of the Americas, and the Atlacatl Battalion, to which they belonged, had received training at Fort Benning" (198).

[24] Rodolfo Cardenal, SJ, "The Continuing Presence of Archbishop Romero," March 20, 2008, www.thinkingfaith.org. "In a society disfigured by violence, massive emigration, inequality and poverty, and the social and political irresponsibility of its leaders, Oscar Romero is still a hugely significant figure."

[25] Oscar Romero *The Violence of Love,* comp. and trans. James Brockman (Maryknoll, NY: Orbis Books; Farmington, PA: Plough Publishing House, 2004), November 18, 1979, homily, 173.

[26] Sobrino, *Archbishop Romero,* 7.

[27] Information on Romero's life is taken from his definitive biography by James Brockman, *Romero: A Life* (Maryknoll, NY: Orbis Books, 1989), 33–61, and Jesus Delgado, *Oscar A. Romero: Biografía* (Madrid: Ediciones Paulinas, 1986), 9–70. See also *Vida de Oscar Romero: 1917–1980* (San Salvador: Equipo Maiz, 2006).

[28] María López Vigil, *Oscar Romero: Memories in Mosaic,* trans. by Kathy Ogle (Washington, DC: EPICA, 2000), testimony of Zaida Romero and Tiberio Arnoldo Romero, 17.

[29] Ibid.

[30] Ibid.

[31] López Vigil, *Oscar Romero: Memories in Mosaic,* testimony of Carmen Chacón, 15–16.

[32] Brockman, *Romero: A Life,* 36, citing Delgado, *Oscar A. Romero,* 11.

[33] Delgado, *Oscar A. Romero,* 22–23.

[34] Brockman, *Romero: A Life,* 37.

[35] Ibid., 39.

[36] Romero, *Chaparrastique,* September 29, 1962, quoted by Delgado, *Oscar A. Romero,* 21, and cited by Brockman, *Romero: A Life,* 38.

[37] Brockman, *Romero: A Life,* 38, citing Delgado, *Oscar A. Romero,* 22.

[38] Romero, February 4, 1943, entry in his diary, cited in Brockman, *Romero: A Life,* 38–39.

[39] Mons. Jesús Delgado, "Romero: Un Joven Aspirante a la Santidad," *Orientación,* March 25, 2007.

[40] Ibid. ( author's translation).

[41] Brockman, *Romero: A Life,* 39.

[42] López Vigil, *Oscar Romero: Memories in Mosaic,* testimony of Moisés González, 17–18.

[43] Brockman, *Romero: A Life,* 39–41.

[44] Later in his life, when he was archbishop, Romero told an interviewer that he would expand this motto to read: "To be of one mind with the

church incarnated in this people which stands in need of liberation." See James Brockman, "The Spiritual Journey of Oscar Romero," and his footnote 14, citing Oscar Romero, "Reflections on the Spiritual Exercises," *The Way*, Supplement 55, Spring 1986, 101.

[45] López Vigil, *Oscar Romero: Memories in Mosaic,* testimony of Raúl Romero, 21.

[46] Ibid., testimony of Elvira Chacón, 23.

[47] Ibid., testimony of Nelly Rodríguez, 22.

[48] Ibid., testimony of Rutilio Sánchez, 26.

[49] Alejandro and his wife, Exaltación, lost three more sons in the war in addition to Octavio, their son the priest who was assassinated.

[50] López Vigil, *Oscar Romero: Memories in Mosaic*, testimony of Alejandro Ortiz, 24–25.

[51] Ibid., testimony of Miguel Vásquez, 28.

[52] Ibid., testimony of Antonia Novoa, 31.

[53] Ibid., 31–32.

[54] Brockman, *Romero: A Life*, 41.

[55] Ibid., 42, citing Delgado, *Oscar A. Romero,* 30–31.

[56] López Vigil, *Oscar Romero: Memories in Mosaic*, testimony of María Varona, 33–34.

[57] Ibid., testimony of Miguel Ventura, 38.

[58] Penny Lernoux, *Cry of the People* (New York: Penguin, 1982), 37.

[59] Ibid., 38.

[60] Ibid., 40.

[61] Ibid., 41.

[62] López Vigil, *Oscar Romero: Memories in Mosaic,* testimony of Salvador Carranza, 37–38.

[63] Brockman, *Romero: A Life*, 45.

[64] Armstrong and Shenk, *El Salvador: The Face of Revolution*, 53–58.

[65] López Vigil, *Oscar Romero: Memories in Mosaic,* testimony of Francisco Estrada, 52–53.

[66] Ibid., testimony of Pedro Declerc and Noemí Ortiz, 47.

[67] For an excellent account of the formation of this community, see Pablo Galdámez, *Faith of a People: The Life of a Basic Christian Community in El Salvador* (Maryknoll, NY: Orbis Books, 1986).

[68] López Vigil, *Oscar Romero: Memories in Mosaic,* testimony of Pedro Declerc and Noemí Ortiz, 49–50.

[69] Brockman, *Romero: A Life,* citing Delgado, *Oscar A. Romero*, 59.

[70] Brockman, *Romero: A Life,* citing Delgado, *Oscar A. Romero,* 60.

[71] Brockman, *Romero: A Life*, 61.

[72] López Vigil, *Oscar Romero: Memories in Mosaic,* testimony of Juan Macho, 71–73.

[73] Brockman, *Romero: A Life,* 60. The book in question was Jon Sobrino, *Christology at the Crossroads* (Maryknoll, NY: Orbis Books, 1978).

[74] López Vigil, *Oscar Romero: Memories in Mosaic,* testimony of Juan Macho, 71–73.

[75] Brockman, *Romero: A Life,* 55.

[76] Zacarías Díez y Juan Macho, *En Santiago de María Me Topé con la Miseria: Dos Años de la Vida de Monseñor Romero* (San Salvador: Pasionistas, 1994), 9–12.

[77] Brockman, *Romero: A Life,* 54.

[78] López Vigil, *Oscar Romero: Memories in Mosaic,* testimony of Rafael Moreno, 69.

[79] Ibid., testimony of Pedro Ferradas, 67–69.

[80] See Rodolfo Cardenal, *Historia de una esperanza: Vida de Rutilio Grande* (San Salvador: UCA Editores, 1985).

[81] Ibid. (author's translation).

[82] López Vigil, *Oscar Romero: Memories in Mosaic,* testimony of Francisco Estrada, 81.

[83] Brockman, *Romero: A Life,* 5.

[84] López Vigil, *Oscar Romero: Memories in Mosaic,* testimony of Ernestina Rivera, 103–4.

[85] *Monseñor Oscar A. Romero, Su Pensamiento* I–II (San Salvador: Publicaciones Pastorales del Arzobispado, 2000), "Homilía en la Misa Exequial del Padre Rutilio Grande," 1–5 (author's translation).

[86] Brockman, *Romero: A Life*, "Letter of Romero to Molina, March 14, 1977," 11.

[87] Brockman, *Romero: A Life*, 15.

[88] López Vigil, *Oscar Romero: Memories in Mosaic,* testimony of César Jerez, 111–12.

[89] Brockman, *Romero: A Life*, cited in *Orientación,* March 27, 1977.

[90] López Vigil, *Oscar Romero: Memories in Mosaic,* testimony of Inocencio Alas, 117–18.

[91] Sobrino, *Archbishop Romero,* 10.

[92] Ignacio Martin-Baro, "Oscar Romero: Voice of the Downtrodden," in *Voice of the Voiceless,* 4.

[93] Maier, *Monseñor Romero: Maestro de espiritualidad*, 100.

[94] Sobrino, *Archbishop Romero,* 7.

95 See Jon Sobrino, *Christ the Liberator* (Maryknoll, NY: Orbis Books, 2001), 12–14, 74–78. This reference is thanks to Kevin Burke, SJ, in his article, "Announcing Resurrection, The Challenge and Gift of Archbishop Romero," paper given at a symposium, "Memory, Prophecy, Hope: The Legacy of the Central American Martyrs," Rivier College, Nashua, New Hampshire, June 14, 2005.

96 Ibid.

97 Sobrino, *Archbishop Romero*, 8–9.

98 Maier, *Monseñor Romero: Maestro de espiritualidad*, 105.

99 López Vigil, *Oscar Romero: Memories in Mosaic*, testimony of César Jerez, 158–59.

100 Ibid., testimony of Ricardo Urioste, 154–55.

101 Brockman, *Romero: A Life*, 20.

102 Oscar Romero, "The Easter Church," in *Voice of the Voiceless*, 59.

103 López Vigil, *Oscar Romero: Memories in Mosaic*, testimony of Teresa Alas, 122.

104 Ibid., testimony of Roberto Cuellar, 125–26.

105 Ibid., testimony of Miguel Vásquez, 140–41.

106 Brockman, *Romero: A Life*, 28–29.

107 Ibid., 29.

108 Ibid.

109 López Vigil, *Oscar Romero: Memories in Mosaic*, testimony of José Luís Ortega, 167–69.

110 Brockman, *Romero: A Life*, 31.

111 Sobrino, *Archbishop Romero*, 26–27.

112 López Vigil, *Oscar Romero: Memories in Mosaic*, testimony of Jon Sobrino, 170–71.

113 Romero: , *The Violence of Love*, July 17, 1977, homily, 5.

114 Brockman, *Romero: A Life*, 80.

115 Oscar Romero, "The Church, Body of Christ in History," in *Voice of the Voiceless*, 65.

116 Jon Sobrino, "El pensamiento doctrinal de Monseñor Romero," in *Cartas Pastorales y Discursos de Monseñor Oscar A. Romero* (San Salvador: Centro Monseñor Romero, 2007), 5 (author's translation).

117 Ibid., 7.

118 Ibid.

119 Romero, "The Church, Body of Christ in History," in *Voice of the Voiceless*, 81.

120 Brockman, *Romero: A Life*, 80, citing Oscar Romero, "The Church, Body of Christ in History."

121 *Justice in the World*, 6.

122 *Medellín*, Justice 1, cited in Romero, "The Church, Body of Christ in History," in *Voice of the Voiceless*, 68.

123 *Medellín*, Poverty 7, cited in Romero, "The Church, Body of Christ in History," in *Voice of the Voiceless*, 66.

124 Paul VI, *Octogesima Adveniens*, 4.

125 Romero, "The Church, Body of Christ in History," in *Voice of the Voiceless*, 81.

126 Brockman, *Romero, A Life*, 84–85.

127 Ibid., 86–87.

128 Ibid., 98–99.

129 Ibid., 99.

130 López Vigil, *Oscar Romero: Memories in Mosaic*, 178.

131 Ibid., testimony of Fabio Argueta, 179–80.

132 Brockman, *Romero: A Life*, 101. See also "La Iglesia de la Esperanza," 27 de noviembre, 1977, *Monseñor Oscar A. Romero, Su Pensamiento* III (San Salvador: Publicaciones Pastorales del Arzobispado, 2000), 3–4.

133 Brockman, *Romero: A Life*, 101.

134 Ibid.,101–2.

135 Romero, *The Violence of Love*, 11–27.

136 In 1993, the State Department was mandated to evaluate U.S. foreign policy with regard to El Salvador, and concluded that these two goals were not in conflict. Such a conclusion reflected the State Department policy during the war of testifying before Congress that human rights had "improved" in El Salvador, thus enabling the Pentagon to continue to send military aid to El Salvador.

137 Oscar Romero, "Georgetown Address," February 14, 1978, in *Voice of the Voiceless*, 161–67.

138 Ibid., 163–64.

139 Ibid., 165.

140 Ibid., 166.

141 Brockman, *Romero: A Life*, 108.

142 López Vigil, *Oscar Romero: Memories in Mosaic*, testimony of Tomasa Pérez, 184.

143 Ibid., testimony of Mariana Alonso, 184.

144 Paul VI, *Octogesima Adveniens*, 4. "It is up to the Christian communities to analyze with objectivity the situation proper to their country, to shed on it the light of the Gospel's unalterable words, and to draw principles of reflection, norms of judgment and directives for action from the social teaching of

the Church."

[145] Oscar Romero, "The Church and Popular Political Organizations," in *Voice of the Voiceless*, 88.

[146] Brockman, *Romero: A Life*, 138, and Sobrino, "El Pensamiento doctrinal de Monseñor Romero," 8–9.

[147] *Medellín*, Peace 20, 27, cited in Romero, "The Church and Popular Political Organizations," in *Voice of the Voiceless*, 93–94.

[148] Romero, "The Church and Popular Political Organizations," in *Voice of the Voiceless*, 97.

[149] Ibid.

[150] Paul VI, *Evangelii Nuntiandi*, 30.

[151] Romero, "The Church and Popular Political Organizations," in *Voice of the Voiceless*, 100.

[152] Ibid., 106–7.

[153] *Medellín*, Peace 15, cited in Romero, "The Church and Popular Political Organizations," in *Voice of the Voiceless*, 109.

[154] Romero, "The Church and Popular Political Organizations," in *Voice of the Voiceless*, 109.

[155] Romero, *The Violence of Love,* October 15, 1978 homily, 95.

[156] Ibid., 96.

[157] Romero, "The Church and Popular Political Organizations," in *Voice of the Voiceless*, 105.

[158] Brockman, *Romero: A Life*, 150–53.

[159] Ibid., 136.

[160] López Vigil, *Oscar Romero: Memories in Mosaic*, testimony of Astor Ruíz, 262–64.

[161] Romero, "The Church and Popular Political Organizations," in *Voice of the Voiceless*, 110.

[162] Romero, *The Violence of Love*, 101–17.

[163] López Vigil, *Oscar Romero: Memories in Mosaic*, testimony of the Community of San Antonio Abad, 282–83.

[164] Ibid., testimony of Carmen Elena Hernández, 283–85.

[165] Ibid., testimony of Alejandro Ortiz, 285–88.

[166] Ibid.

[167] Ibid., 288.

[168] Brockman, *Romero: A Life*, 156.

[169] Ibid.

[170] Ibid., 159–60.

[171] Ibid., 160.

[172] Maier, *Monseñor Romero: Maestro de espiritualidad*, 101.

[173] Brockman, *Romero: A Life*, 162, citing a text from Romero's files.

[174] Brockman, *Romero: A Life,* 161, citing the letter dated February 10, 1979.

[175] López Vigil, *Oscar Romero: Memories in Mosaic*, testimony of María del Carmen Pérez, 244–45.

[176] Brockman, *Romero: A Life*, 164, citing *Monseñor Oscar A. Romero: Su Pensamiento* VI, 157–59.

[177] Brockman, *Romero: A Life*, 167.

[178] López Vigil, *Oscar Romero: Memories in Mosaic*, 302–6. María López Vigil, who narrates this scene, adds: "Monseñor Romero told me all this, practically in tears, on May 11, 1979, in Madrid when he was hurrying back to his country, wracked with worry about the news of a killing in the Cathedral in San Salvador."

[179] Brockman, *Romero: A Life*, 171, and López Vigil, *Oscar Romero: Memories in Mosaic*, 306.

[180] Brockman, *Romero: A Life*, 177, citing *Monseñor Oscar A. Romero: Su Pensamiento* VII, 35–37.

[181] Brockman, *Romero: A Life*, 181–82.

[182] Sobrino, "El pensamiento doctrinal de Monseñor Romero," 9–10 (author's translation).

[183] Paul VI, *Octogesima Adveniens* 4.

[184] *Puebla*, 89.

[185] *Puebla*, 31–39.

[186] Romero, "The Church's Mission amid the National Crisis," in *Voice of the Voiceless*, 121–22.

[187] Ibid., 122.

[188] Ibid., 138.

[189] Ibid., 138.

[190] Ibid., 154–55.

[191] Brockman, *Romero: A Life*, 184.

[192] Ibid., 185.

[193] Ibid., 194.

[194] Ibid.

[195] Brockman, *Romero: A Life*, 198, citing Delgado, *Oscar A. Romero*, 151.

[196] Brockman, *Romero: A Life,* 195.

[197] López Vigil, *Oscar Romero: Memories in Mosaic*, testimony of Pedrina Gómez, 317–19.

[198] Ibid., testimony of Juan Bosco Palacios and Antonio Cardenal, 325–26.

[199] Brockman, *Romero: A Life*, 198.

[200] López Vigil, *Oscar Romero: Memories in Mosaic*, testimony of Carmen Elena Hernández, 334–36.

[201] Brockman, *Romero: A Life*, 214.

[202] Ibid., 215.

[203] Ibid., 218.

[204] Ibid., 219.

[205] Romero, *The Violence of Love*, 176–79.

[206] *Monseñor Oscar A. Romero: Su Pensamiento* VIII (San Salvador: Publicaciones Pastorales del Arzobispado, 2000), excerpts from Romero's Epiphany homily, January 6, 1980, trans. Sally Hanlon.

[207] Brockman, *Romero: A Life*, 219.

[208] Ibid., 220.

[209] Ibid.

[210] López Vigil, *Oscar Romero: Memories in Mosaic*, testimony of Jacinto Bustillo, 368–69.

[211] Brockman, *Romero: A Life*, 222–23.

[212] Archbishop Oscar Romero, *A Shepherd's Diary*, trans. Irene B. Hodgson (Washington, DC: United States Catholic Conference, 1993), 466.

[213] Brockman, *Romero: A Life*, 224–25.

[214] Romero, "The Political Dimension of the Faith from the Perspective of the Option for the Poor," in *Voice of the Voiceless*, 179.

[215] Ibid.

[216] Ibid., 179–80.

[217] Ibid., 180.

[218] Ibid., 180–81.

[219] Ibid., 181.

[220] Ibid.

[221] Ibid., 182.

[222] Ibid.

[223] Ibid., 185.

[224] Brockman, *Romero: A Life*, 227.

[225] Brian Pierce, OP, "The Heart of Being Neighbor: Oscar Romero, Preacher," *Central America Report* (Washington, DC: Religious Task Force on Central America and Mexico, 2005), March/April 2005.

[226] López Vigil, *Oscar Romero: Memories in Mosaic*, testimony of Rafael Urrutia, 224–25.

[227] Romero, *The Violence of Love*, February 17, 1980, homily, 191.

[228] Ibid., 191–92.

[229] *Monseñor Oscar A. Romero: Su Pensamiento*, September 3, 1978, homily. See also Miguel Cavada Diez, *Predicación y Profecía: Análisis de las Homilías de Monseñor Romero* (San Salvador: UCA Editores, 1993), Master's thesis. Author's translation.

[230] *Monseñor Oscar A. Romero, Su Pensamiento*, July 8, 1979, homily.

[231] Ibid., July 16, 1978, homily.

[232] Ibid., November 11, 1979, homily.

[233] Ibid., January 27, 1980, homily.

[234] Brockman, *Romero: A Life*, 233.

[235] Ibid., 234.

[236] Ibid., 235.

[237] Romero, *The Violence of Love*, March 2, 1980, homily, 196–97.

[238] Brockman, *Romero: A Life*, 236–37, citing Romero's March 9, 1980, homily.

[239] López Vigil, *Oscar Romero: Memories in Mosaic*, testimony of Francisco Román, 387–88.

[240] Romero, *The Violence of Love*, March 16, 1980 homily, 200.

[241] López Vigil, *Oscar Romero: Memories in Mosaic*, testimony of Rafael Moreno and Rutilio Sánchez, 379–80.

[242] Ibid., 380.

[243] Romero, *La voz de los sin voz*, March 1980 interview, 461. Author's translation.

[244] Oscar Romero, "A Pastor's Last Homily," *Sojourners Magazine* (May 1980): 12, translation of Romero's March 23, 1980, homily.

[245] Romero, "A Pastor's Last Homily," 12–13.

[246] Ibid., 14.

[247] Ibid., 15.

[248] Ibid., 15–16.

[249] Ibid., 16.

[250] Romero, *La voz de los sin voz*, March 1980 interview, 461.

[251] The United Nations Truth Commission for El Salvador and the Inter-American Commission on Human Rights both concluded after separate investigations that Alvaro Rafael Saravia was actively involved in planning and carrying out the assassination. In September 2003, the Center for Justice and Accountability filed a lawsuit against Saravia in the federal district court in Fresno, California, alleging that he obtained weapons and vehicles to carry out the assassination, provided his personal driver to transport the assassin to and from the chapel where Romero was shot, and paid the assassin after the assassination had been carried out. Saravia later advised death squad leader Roberto D'Aubuisson, with whom he worked closely, that the plan to carry out the assassination had been successfully completed. Judge Oliver Wanger of the

federal district court in Fresno subsequently found Saravia liable for Romero's assassination, and Saravia was ordered to pay $10 million to the plaintiff, a relative of Archbishop Romero. The identity of the actual assassin has never been discovered.

252 *Monseñor Oscar A. Romero: Su pensamiento*, VIII, 383–84, March 24, 1980, homily.

253 Sobrino, *Archbishop Romero*, 41.

254 Romero, *The Violence of Love*, July 15, 1979, homily, 146–47.

255 *Gaudium et spes,* 1.

256 Sobrino, *Archbishop Romero*, 38.

257 Romero, "The Political Dimension of the Faith from the Perspective of the Option for the Poor," in *Voice of the Voiceless*, 182.

258 Ibid.

259 Romero, *La voz de los sin voz*, March 1980, 461.

260 Tertullian.

261 *Carta a las Iglesias*, no. 206.

262 Ibid.

263 Ibid.

264 Ibid.

265 Ibid., no. 48.

266 Ibid., no. 89.

267 Ibid., no. 206.

268 Ibid., no. 326.

269 Ibid.

270 Ibid., no. 373.

271 Ibid., no. 350.

272 Jon Sobrino, "Helping Jesus' Legacy to Bear Fruit in the Churches: Ellacuría on Archbishop Romero," in Jon Sobrino, *No Salvation Outside the Poor: Prophetic-Utopian Essays* (Maryknoll, NY: Orbis Books, 2008), 126.

273 *Carta a las Iglesias,* no. 254.

274 People came from Asia, Australia, Africa, Latin America, Europe, and the United States. SICSAL (Servicio Internacional Cristiano en Solidaridad con los Pueblos de America Latina "Oscar Romero"), a network of faith-based communities in solidarity with Latin America, was also present, and celebrated its twenty-fifth anniversary as well. For more information, see www.sicsal.net and www.sicsal-usa.org.

275 Kevin Dowling, "Remembering Archbishop Romero in a Time of Global Apartheid," in *Central America Report*, March/April 2005, 12–13.

276 Ibid.

277 Ibid.

278 Ibid.

279 Ibid.

280 Ibid.

281 Johnson, *Friends of God and Prophets,* 7–8.

282 Ibid., 243.

283 Johnson, *Friends of God and Prophets*, 23. See also Johann Baptist Metz, *Faith in History and Society* (New York: Seabury, 1980), especially "The Dangerous Memory of the Freedom of Jesus Christ," 88–99; "The Future in the Memory of Suffering," 100–118; and "Categories: Memory, Narrative, Solidarity," 184–237.

284 Johnson, *Friends of God and Prophets*, 168.

285 Ibid., 165.

286 Ibid., 176.

287 The ten martyrs were Oscar Romero of El Salvador; Dietrich Bonhoeffer of Germany; Martin Luther King, Jr., of the United States; Maximilian Kolbe of Poland; Janani Luwum of Uganda; Grand Duchess Elizabeth of Russia; Manche Masemola of South Africa; Lucian Tapiedi of Papua, New Guinea; Esther John of Pakistan; and Wang Zhiming of China.

288 Geffrey B. Kelly and F. Burton Nelson, *The Cost of Moral Leadership: The Spirituality of Dietrich Bonhoeffer* (Grand Rapids, MI: Wm. B. Eerdmans, 2003).

289 Ibid., 44–45.

290 Ibid., 123.

291 Martin Luther King, Jr., "A Time to Break Silence," in *A Testament of Hope: The Essential Writings of Martin Luther King, Jr.*, ed. James M. Washington (San Francisco: Harper and Row, 1986), 241–43.

292 Kelly and Burton, *The Cost of Moral Leadership*, 123. See Romero, "The Church's Mission amid the National Crisis," in *Voice of the Voiceless*, 134–35, and *Puebla*, No. 549.

293 Albert Camus in an address to the Dominican community in France, 1948.

294 *Monseñor Oscar A. Romero: Su Pensamiento*, December 17, 1978, homily (author's translation).

295 *The National Catholic Reporter*, March 28, 2004.

296 See Regis Armstrong, OFM. Cap., "The Peace Prayer: Three Studies," in *Greyfriars Review*, vol.

10, no. 3, 235–68. The three studies are by Frieder Schulz, "The So-Called Prayer of St. Francis"; Willibrord-Christiaan van Dijk, OFM. Cap., "A Prayer in Search of an Author"; and Jerome Poulenc, OFM, "The Modern Inspiration for the Prayer, 'Lord, Make Me an Instrument of Your Peace.'"

[297] *The National Catholic Reporter*, March 28, 2004. Bishop Gumbleton, whose life, like that of Oscar Romero, has been one dedicated to a Gospel witness for justice and peace, concluded his reflection with these words:

> The reign of God is breaking forth. God is always doing something new. I hope we remember that as we look into our hearts today and discover our sinfulness. God will do something new and heal us, forgive us, send us forth renewed, rededicated, recommitted to doing God's work.
>
> God is always doing something new . . . It's a newness without end. It's the new life of living with God forever . . .

That knowledge should give us a sense of joy and peace similar to what the prophet Isaiah felt when he cried out: "Do not dwell on the past. Do not remember the things of old. Look! God is doing a new thing. Now it springs forth. Do you not see it?"

[298] See Bishop Samuel Ruíz, homily at the thirtieth anniversary of Romero's martyrdom, 2010. *Carta a las Iglesias* (San Salvador: UCA, 2010).

[299] See Martin Maier, SJ, "The Last Shall Be First: Oscar Romero and the Joy of the Gospel," Archbishop Romero Trust Lenten address in London, March 2014.

[300] Jon Sobrino, "Monseñor Romero, dichoso," in *Carta a las Iglesias* (San Salvador, UCA, no. 661, May 1–31, 2015)

[301] These words were pronounced by members of the School of the Americas Watch, March 19, 2013.

[302] See Dean Brackley, S.J., "Meeting the Victim, Loving the Poor," *America*, October 19, 2011.

## Also of interest

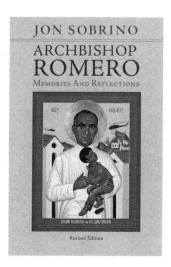

| **Archbishop Romero** | **Monseñor Romero** |
|---|---|
| *Memories and Reflections* | *Memories in Mosaic* |
| Jon Sobrino | Maria López Vigil |

In a moving personal memoir, Salvadoran Jesuit Jon Sobrino describes how Romero emerged as the outspoken champion of the poor and suffering people of El Salvador. He then places Romero in the context of the wider church: as believer, as archbishop, as Salvadoran, as prophet, as martyr, as inspiration for theology. Sobrino sums up his reflections with the conclusion: "Archbishop Romero was a gospel . . . a piece of good news from God to the poor of the world."

ISBN 978-1-62698-176-8 softcover 256pp.

A journalist offers a collective portrait of El Salvador's most beloved pastor, assembled from hundreds of hours of interviews by a journalist with peasants, pastoral workers, theologians, and friends. Together, they describe the archbishop in three dimensions—not as the legendary hero, or the distant saint and martyr, but as a human being with doubts and frailties who found the courage to listen to others, examine his beliefs, and step forward into a role that only he could play.

ISBN 978-1-62698-010-5 softcover 320pp.

Orbis Books, Box 302
Maryknoll, NY 10545-0302
www.orbisbooks.com

# More Books on Oscar Romero
## by James R. Brockman, S.J.

Three short years transformed Archbishop Oscar Romero from a conservative defender of the status quo into one of the church's most outspoken voices of the oppressed. Though silenced by an assassin's bullet, his spirit—and the challenge of his life—lives on. He was beatified by Pope Francis in 2015.

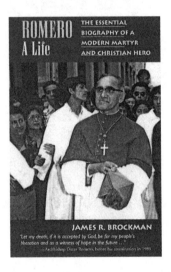

## The Violence of Love

These selections from the sermons and writings of the martyred Archbishop Oscar Romero of El Salvador share the message of a holy prophet of modern times.

ISBN 978-2-57075-535-4 softcover 232pp.

## Romero: A Life

This biography by James Brockman remains the definitive portrait of the modern hero and martyr who became "a voice of the voiceless."

ISBN 978-1-57075-599-6 softcover 296pp.

Orbis Books, Box 302
Maryknoll, NY 10545-0302
www.orbisbooks.com